The Complete Diverticulitis Cookbook

The 3-Stage Meal Plan to Calm Flare-Ups and Heal Your Gut with Simple, Soothing, and Flavorful Recipes

SOFIAH SHAW

Published by
GRAPEVINE BOOKS

www.grapevinebooks.com
email: contact@grapevinebooks.com

Ordering Information:
Quantity sales: Special discounts are available on quantity purchases
by corporations, associations, and others.
For details, reach out to the publisher.

First published by Grapevine Books, 2026

Contents

INTRODUCTION 5

CHAPTER 1: SYMPTOMS, CAUSES, AND DIET FOUNDATIONS 6
UNDERSTANDING FLARE UPS AND THE ROLE OF DIET 6
SYMPTOMS AND CAUSES 6
PREVENTION AND MANAGEMENT 7
BEST SUPPLEMENTS AND NATURAL REMEDIES 7
NAVIGATING DIVERTICULITIS 8
MEDICAL MANAGEMENT 9
DIETARY FUNDAMENTALS 9

CHAPTER 2 PHASE 1: CLEAR LIQUID DIET RECIPES 11
BREAKFAST RECIPES 11
LUNCH RECIPES 14
DINNER RECIPES 17
SNACK RECIPES 20

CHAPTER 3 PHASE 2: LOW FIBER RECOVERY RECIPES 23
BREAKFAST RECIPES 23
LUNCH RECIPES 30
DINNER RECIPES 36
SNACK AND DESSERT RECIPES 40

CHAPTER 4 PHASE 3: HIGH FIBER DIET RECIPES 46
BREAKFAST RECIPES 46
LUNCH RECIPES 54
DINNER RECIPES 61
SNACK AND DESSERT RECIPES 67

CHAPTER 5 INTRODUCTION TO THE 31 DAY MEAL PLAN 74
DAYS 1-3: CLEAR LIQUID PHASE 74
DAYS 4-17: LOW FIBER RECOVERY PHASE 75
DAYS 18-31: HIGH FIBER MAINTENANCE PHASE 78
MOVING FORWARD AFTER THE 31 DAY PLAN 81

CHAPTER 6 BONUS TOOLS FOR DAILY SUPPORT 82
SYMPTOM AND FOOD DIARY 82
WEEKLY SHOPPING LISTS 82
FIBER REINTRODUCTION GUIDE 83
MEAL PREP TIPS FOR COMFORT 84
GENTLE LIFESTYLE HABITS 84

INTRODUCTION

Understanding the basics of diverticular disease helps you approach this condition with clarity rather than uncertainty. Learning how diverticula form, how diverticulitis develops, and how flare ups behave allows you to respond to symptoms with greater confidence.

Diverticula are small pouch-like structures that may appear along the lining of the colon over time. Their presence alone is known as diverticulosis, a condition that often causes no symptoms at all. When one or more of these sacs become inflamed or irritated, diverticulitis occurs. This shift can introduce abdominal pain, digestive changes, and other discomforts that require careful attention. Although flare ups can feel overwhelming, understanding what triggers them makes it easier to manage the condition effectively.

Diet plays a key role throughout this process. During a flare, lighter foods may help calm irritation, while a more structured, fiber focused pattern supports long term stability. With the right approach, you can learn to reduce flare ups, support your digestive system, and create habits that promote steady comfort over time. This guide will walk you through these steps and help you feel more in control of your digestive well being.

CHAPTER 1: SYMPTOMS, CAUSES, AND DIET FOUNDATIONS

UNDERSTANDING FLARE UPS AND THE ROLE OF DIET

Flare ups can seem unpredictable at first, but they follow patterns that become easier to recognize as you learn more about how diverticulitis behaves. Understanding why the body reacts the way it does can help you approach these moments with more clarity and less fear.

A flare typically begins when one of the diverticular pouches becomes irritated or obstructed. When this happens, the surrounding tissue may swell and become inflamed, which leads to the discomfort commonly associated with diverticulitis. The digestive tract is sensitive to changes like these, so even a small amount of inflammation can disrupt how the bowel moves and processes food. This is why flare ups often come with noticeable shifts in digestion, energy levels, and appetite.

Diet plays a meaningful role during this stage. When inflammation is present, the digestive system benefits from reduced workload. Clear liquids and simple broths provide hydration without adding strain, allowing the intestines to rest. This period of bowel rest is often short but important, as it gives the inflamed tissue time to settle. As symptoms improve, soft foods help transition the body back to gentle digestion before gradually introducing more substantial foods. This slow progression reduces irritation and lowers the risk of prolonging the flare.

Once healing begins, a well structured eating pattern becomes a valuable tool for long term comfort. Balanced fiber intake, regular hydration, and consistent meals help soften stools and maintain steady movement through the colon. These habits reduce internal pressure, which may lower the likelihood of diverticula becoming irritated again. Over time, many individuals find that dietary awareness becomes one of their strongest allies in preventing future episodes and maintaining day to day digestive ease.

SYMPTOMS AND CAUSES

Recognizing the symptoms of diverticulitis can help you identify flare ups sooner, which often leads to more effective management. Although symptoms vary slightly from person to person, several common warning signs point to irritation or inflammation within the colon. Paying attention to these early changes can prevent symptoms from escalating and can help you respond before discomfort becomes severe.

Persistent abdominal pain is the symptom most closely linked with diverticulitis. This discomfort is often sharp and steady and is usually felt on the lower left side of the abdomen. However, pain can occur on the right side or across the entire lower abdomen depending on which diverticulum is affected. The pain may worsen when bending forward, lifting objects, coughing, or applying pressure to the stomach region. As inflammation progresses, the body may produce fever or chills as part of its natural defense response, signaling that the immune system is working harder to address the irritation.

Digestive changes also provide important clues that a flare up may be developing. Constipation is common because inflammation makes it harder for the colon to move stool smoothly along its pathway. Some people notice loose stools instead, or a cycle of alternating constipation and diarrhea as the bowel struggles to regulate itself. Bloating and excess gas can be uncomfortable reminders that the colon is not functioning normally. A sensation of fullness after small meals or even between meals can occur because the digestive system becomes more sensitive during inflammation. Nausea and vomiting may develop when swelling disrupts normal digestive movement or suppresses appetite. Fatigue and loss of appetite are also frequent, especially when eating increases discomfort or when the body is using extra energy to handle inflammation.

Several factors contribute to the development of diverticulitis. Age related changes naturally weaken the structure of the colon over time, making small pockets more likely to form. Genetic tendencies also play a role, especially when close family members have experienced diverticulosis or diverticulitis. Diets that are consistently low in fiber can cause stools to become dense or difficult to pass, which increases internal pressure and encourages the formation of diverticula. Inadequate hydration affects stool softness and contributes to irregular bowel habits, further stressing the colon.

Lifestyle habits influence risk as well. A sedentary routine slows digestion, and reduced movement can lead to constipation, which increases strain on the intestinal walls. Carrying excess weight raises abdominal pressure and may worsen inflammation. Smoking interferes with blood flow and the body's natural healing processes, which may make flare ups more likely or more intense. Certain medications, including some pain relievers, steroids, or anti-inflammatory drugs, can irritate the digestive lining or alter the immune response in ways that raise sensitivity in the colon.

Understanding these influences helps build a clearer foundation for prevention. Some risk factors, such as age or genetics, cannot be changed, but many can be improved through thoughtful adjustments to diet, hydration, movement, and daily habits. Identifying which triggers relate to your personal health allows you to make practical choices that support long term digestive comfort and reduce the likelihood of future flare ups.

PREVENTION AND MANAGEMENT

Preventing diverticulitis flare ups becomes much easier when you understand how daily habits influence the health of the colon. While no single adjustment can guarantee complete protection, a combination of supportive routines can significantly lower the likelihood of inflammation.

One of the most effective strategies is maintaining steady bowel habits. When stools remain soft and pass comfortably, pressure inside the colon decreases. This reduced pressure helps protect the diverticular pouches from irritation. A well balanced diet that includes fiber once the digestive system is stable can support this process by promoting regularity. Hydration is equally important, as water softens stool and encourages smoother movement through the intestines.

Movement also plays a meaningful role in prevention. Regular physical activity helps stimulate natural bowel motions and reduces the risk of sluggish digestion. Even simple routines such as daily walking can have noticeable benefits over time. In addition to aiding digestion, gentle activity supports overall circulation and can contribute to a greater sense of well being.

Weight management is another helpful factor. Carrying excess weight, especially around the abdomen, can increase pressure within the digestive tract. Over time, this added strain may contribute to inflammation. A balanced approach to nutrition and activity supports a healthier weight and lowers the chances of future flare ups.

Avoiding habits that irritate the digestive tract can further support prevention. Smoking is known to weaken natural healing responses and may heighten inflammation in the colon. Certain medications, such as specific anti inflammatory drugs, may also irritate the gastrointestinal lining. If you rely on medications regularly, discuss suitable alternatives or modifications with your healthcare provider.

During periods when the digestive system feels unsettled, making temporary adjustments to diet can help calm symptoms before they escalate. Choosing easier to digest foods, limiting heavy or highly processed items, and paying attention to early warning signs can make a difference in stopping a flare before it deepens. Long term prevention often comes down to consistency. When supportive habits become part of daily life, the colon can function with greater ease and resilience.

BEST SUPPLEMENTS AND NATURAL REMEDIES

Many individuals find relief and improved digestive comfort by incorporating certain supplements and natural remedies into their daily routine. While these options should not replace professional medical care, they can offer meaningful support when used thoughtfully and with proper guidance. Understanding how each remedy works allows you to choose those that best match your body's needs and long term goals.

Probiotics remain one of the most frequently recommended supplements for digestive wellness. These beneficial bacteria help maintain a balanced gut environment, which can contribute to reduced inflammation and more predictable digestion. A well supported microbiome may help the colon respond more calmly to stress and irritation. Probiotics are available in multiple forms, including capsules, powders, and fermented foods such as yogurt or kefir, provided they are well tolerated. Choosing a reputable brand and starting with a gentle formula can help the body adjust gradually.

Fiber supplements can also play a helpful role in maintaining long term stability, although they should only be introduced once active inflammation has completely settled. Options that contain soluble fiber, such as psyllium husk, help soften stools and encourage regularity by absorbing water and adding gentle bulk. Proper hydration is essential for these supplements to work effectively. Introducing fiber slowly allows the digestive system to adapt and reduces the likelihood of gas or bloating as the body adjusts to the increased intake.

Some individuals find value in herbal remedies that offer natural soothing effects. Peppermint is often used to ease mild cramping or abdominal tightness. Chamomile can promote relaxation and may help calm general digestive discomfort. Ginger provides gentle support for nausea or sluggish digestion. When considering herbal supplements, quality matters, and it is wise to consult a healthcare provider before including them in your routine. This helps ensure that the products chosen are safe and suitable for your unique health profile.

Daily hydration can be one of the most effective natural tools for digestive comfort. Drinking enough water helps maintain stool softness and keeps the digestive system functioning with less strain. Warm liquids such as mild herbal teas or warm lemon water may provide additional comfort by encouraging smoother movement through the intestines. Consistency is key, as regular hydration supports overall digestive resilience.

Magnesium is another supplement that may benefit those who struggle with slower bowel movements. Certain forms of magnesium, particularly magnesium citrate or magnesium glycinate, can support the natural rhythm of the intestines by helping the muscles relax. Selecting the right form and appropriate dose is important, as the effects can vary from person to person. Gentle, steady use under professional supervision tends to yield the most predictable results.

When combined with balanced eating patterns, steady hydration, physical activity, and regular medical check ins, these supplements and natural remedies can provide an added layer of support. They work best when used as part of a comprehensive and mindful approach to digestive health.

NAVIGATING DIVERTICULITIS

Living with diverticulitis becomes far more manageable when you understand how the condition behaves through its different stages. Each phase places different demands on the digestive system, and knowing how to respond helps you reduce discomfort, avoid complications, and build confidence in your daily routine. With a clear sense of what your body needs at each step, diverticulitis becomes a condition you can actively manage rather than something that disrupts your life unexpectedly.

During a flare up, the primary goal is to calm inflammation and minimize strain on the colon. When the digestive tract is irritated, foods that require substantial breakdown can worsen symptoms. This is why clear liquids, simple broths, gelatin, herbal teas, and electrolyte rich fluids form the foundation of early flare management. These choices help maintain hydration and give the intestines essential rest. This stage is usually short, but it has a powerful impact on how quickly the flare resolves. Paying close attention to changing symptoms can help you decide when you are ready to move forward. A decrease in sharp abdominal pain and improvement in bloating or nausea often signal that the digestive tract is settling.

As the flare begins to ease, the next stage involves reintroducing soft, low fiber foods. These choices act as a bridge between liquids and regular eating. Foods such as mashed potatoes, smooth rice porridge, soft eggs, plain pasta, tender white fish, and other mild, easy to digest options allow the digestive system to re-engage gradually. This transition helps prevent unnecessary irritation during a vulnerable period. Eating smaller meals, chewing thoroughly, and allowing adequate time between meals support healing by reducing digestive workload.

Once symptoms resolve fully, the focus shifts toward long term prevention. This stage is where balanced, fiber rich eating becomes essential. Fiber adds softness and bulk to stool, helps regulate bowel movements, and lowers internal pressure within the colon. These effects make future flare ups less likely. The key is to add fiber slowly and steadily. Gradual increases in whole grains, cooked vegetables, fruits, legumes, and seeds help the body adjust without new discomfort. Hydration is equally important, since fiber works best when paired with ample water.

Navigating diverticulitis also includes tuning in to early signals from your body. Subtle shifts such as reduced appetite, mild cramping, fatigue, or changes in bowel habits may indicate that the digestive system needs extra care. Addressing these signs early can stop a small irritation from progressing into a full flare. Keeping a simple journal of foods eaten, symptoms experienced, stress levels, sleep patterns, and physical activity can help reveal patterns that influence digestive comfort.

Although diverticulitis can feel unpredictable, understanding the stages and responding intentionally at each point brings greater stability. With patience, awareness, and consistent daily habits, many individuals discover that they can reduce flare frequency, improve overall comfort, and regain a sense of control in their daily lives.

MEDICAL MANAGEMENT

Medical care forms an essential part of managing diverticulitis, particularly during active flare ups or when symptoms become more concerning. Knowing when to seek medical attention and understanding the available treatment options can help you respond quickly and confidently when discomfort begins. Early evaluation allows healthcare providers to distinguish between mild inflammation and more complex situations that require closer supervision.

When symptoms first appear, a healthcare provider typically begins with a physical examination and a discussion of recent changes in digestion or pain. Blood tests may be used to check markers of inflammation or infection, and imaging studies such as a CT scan can help identify the exact location and severity of the flare. These steps offer a clear picture of how the colon is functioning and whether complications are beginning to form. Mild cases are often treated at home with rest, hydration, and dietary adjustments, along with careful monitoring for any signs of worsening.

In some situations, medication becomes necessary to support healing. Antibiotics may be recommended when there is evidence of infection or when risk factors make complications more likely. These medications help reduce harmful bacterial activity that can intensify inflammation. Not all flare ups require antibiotics, and the decision is made based on individual symptoms and overall medical history. Pain relief may also be prescribed, but only from medications that are gentle on the digestive tract. Options are chosen thoughtfully to avoid irritating the colon or slowing its healing process.

More severe flare ups may require hospital care, particularly if symptoms accelerate or if eating and drinking become difficult. In these cases, intravenous fluids restore hydration and prevent further strain on the digestive system. Medications given through an IV can help calm inflammation more quickly, while rest allows the colon to recover. Most individuals respond well to this short period of hospital management and can gradually resume normal activity as symptoms improve.

Surgery is reserved for situations where complications arise or when repeated flare ups significantly interfere with daily life. This may include conditions such as abscesses, blockages, or small tears in the colon wall. Modern surgical techniques are more precise and less invasive than in the past, which helps reduce recovery time and improves long term outcomes. If surgery becomes a possibility, healthcare providers explain the reasons, potential benefits, and steps involved so you can make informed decisions with confidence.

Ongoing follow up care helps maintain stability after a flare. These appointments allow healthcare providers to review diet, symptoms, activity habits, and any new concerns. This regular communication helps catch small issues early and reinforces supportive routines that protect the colon from future inflammation. With a combination of medical guidance, thoughtful lifestyle choices, and careful monitoring, many individuals manage diverticulitis successfully and enjoy long periods of comfort and normal activity.

DIETARY FUNDAMENTALS

Understanding how diet influences diverticulitis is one of the most important steps toward creating long term digestive comfort. Every food choice shapes how the colon responds, and a steady, supportive eating pattern can significantly reduce the strain placed on the digestive tract. By learning how different foods behave during flare ups and recovery, you can make choices that protect and strengthen your colon over time.

When symptoms first emerge, the digestive tract becomes highly sensitive and may have difficulty processing foods that require effort to break down. For this reason, clear liquids and simple broths are commonly recommended during the earliest stage of discomfort. These options maintain hydration while allowing the colon to rest. As inflammation begins to settle, soft, low fiber foods offer gentle nourishment. Smooth cereals, mashed potatoes, pureed vegetables, and tender proteins supply energy without irritating the affected area. They help bridge the transition between liquid intake and more substantial meals so the digestive system can gradually regain strength.

As recovery continues, slowly reintroducing fiber plays a key role in restoring digestive balance. Fiber absorbs water, softens stool, and encourages easier movement through the colon. This process helps reduce internal pressure, which can lower the risk of future flare ups. Because the colon may still be sensitive, it is best to increase fiber intake gradually. Introducing it too quickly may cause gas or bloating, especially if hydration is not consistent. Drinking enough water helps fiber perform its job more effectively, creating a smoother and more predictable digestive rhythm.

A balanced approach to everyday eating supports overall digestive health. Incorporating cooked vegetables, whole grains, lean proteins, and fruits that are easy to tolerate provides steady nourishment and keeps the digestive tract working comfortably. Cooked vegetables tend to be easier on the intestines than raw ones during the early stages of recovery, since heat softens their fiber. Lean meats and fish offer protein without adding heaviness, while gentle fruits can restore natural sweetness to meals. As tolerance improves, gradually adding more whole foods leads to long term strength and stability.

Meal timing plays a meaningful role as well. Eating smaller, more frequent meals can help reduce pressure on the colon compared to consuming large portions at once. This approach allows the digestive system to process food evenly throughout the day. Paying attention to your body's signals and noticing how different foods affect your comfort can guide your choices. Over time, these patterns become a personalized routine that supports both digestive health and overall well being.

These dietary fundamentals create a strong foundation for managing diverticulitis. With thoughtful adjustments and consistent habits, the digestive system becomes more resilient. While each person's tolerance may vary, a mindful approach to food helps reduce flare ups, supports healing, and promotes stability for the long term.

CHAPTER 2

PHASE 1: CLEAR LIQUID DIET RECIPES

The clear liquid phase is the most temporary part of the diverticulitis diet, yet it plays a meaningful role in calming inflammation. During a flare, the digestive tract benefits from rest, and clear liquids provide hydration and gentle nourishment without forcing the intestines to process solid foods. This brief stage allows irritated tissue to settle and supports the transition into the next phase of recovery.

Clear liquids should feel soothing and easy on the stomach. Broths, clear juices, herbal teas, and lightly flavored beverages help maintain energy and fluid balance while keeping the digestive workload low. Although this stage is limited, choosing liquids that are warm, mild, and uncomplicated can make you more comfortable while symptoms ease. Once sharp pain decreases and digestion feels more settled, you can begin moving to soft, low fiber foods in Phase 2.

The following recipes offer simple, comforting options appropriate for the clear liquid stage. Each one is designed to be gentle, hydrating, and supportive as the body begins to heal.

BREAKFAST RECIPES

Apple Cinnamon Clear Infusion

A warm, fragrant broth that brings mild sweetness without heaviness.

Ingredients

2 cups water

1 cinnamon stick

½ cup clear apple juice

Instructions

Begin by placing the water and cinnamon stick into a small pot and bringing it slowly to a gentle boil. As the water heats, the cinnamon begins to soften and release its natural aroma, creating a soothing infusion. Once it reaches a light boil, lower the heat to a soft simmer and allow the cinnamon to steep for five minutes. This brief simmering time helps the flavor develop without becoming too strong or overpowering.

After the cinnamon has infused the water, stir in the clear apple juice and let the mixture warm through for another moment. The apple juice blends smoothly with the cinnamon infusion, adding a mild sweetness while keeping the liquid light and easy to digest. Once warmed, remove the cinnamon stick and strain the infusion to ensure a smooth, clear drink. Pour into a cup and enjoy warm for gentle comfort during the clear liquid phase.

Warm Lemon Honey Water

A simple drink that soothes the stomach and supports hydration.

Ingredients

1 cup warm water

1 teaspoon lemon juice

½ teaspoon honey

Instructions

Begin by warming the water to a gentle, comfortable temperature that is easy to sip without causing irritation. Add the lemon juice to the warm water and stir briefly, allowing it to disperse evenly and brighten the flavor. The warm water helps soften the acidity of the lemon so it feels soothing rather than sharp, making it suitable for moments when your stomach needs calm support.

Add the honey and continue stirring until it fully dissolves into the mixture. The honey adds a soft sweetness that balances the lemon and provides a smooth, coating warmth as you drink. Once the mixture is fully blended, sip it slowly in small, relaxed sips. This gentle pace helps the drink settle comfortably in your stomach while supporting hydration and easing mild digestive discomfort.

Clear Apple Juice Variation

Light, mild, and easy to digest.

Ingredients

1 cup diluted clear apple juice

½ cup warm water

Instructions

Combine, warm gently if desired, and serve.

White Grape Juice Blend

A gentle alternative for those sensitive to apple-based drinks.

Ingredients

1 cup clear white grape juice

½ cup water

Instructions

Mix, warm lightly if preferred, and drink while comfortable.

Peppermint Herbal Tea

Helps calm bloating and gas while delivering a refreshing flavor.

Ingredients

1 peppermint tea bag

1 cup hot water

Instructions

Place the peppermint tea bag into a mug and pour the hot water over it, allowing the leaves to release their natural oils and aroma. As the tea steeps, the peppermint gradually infuses the water with a clean, refreshing scent that supports relaxation in the digestive tract. Let it sit undisturbed for about five minutes so the flavor becomes smooth and full without becoming too strong for sensitive stomachs.

After steeping, remove the tea bag and let the tea cool slightly until it reaches a comfortable sipping temperature. Peppermint is known for its gentle ability to ease bloating, reduce gas, and calm mild cramping, making this warm drink especially helpful during the clear liquid phase. Sip slowly and allow the warmth and soothing flavor to settle your stomach and promote comfort.

LUNCH RECIPES

Chicken Broth With Fresh Herbs

A classic clear liquid option that feels satisfying without heaviness.

Ingredients

4 pounds chicken pieces

1 large onion, quartered

4 unpeeled garlic cloves

2 large carrots

2 celery stalks, cut into thirds

Small bunch fresh parsley

1 teaspoon whole peppercorns

Salt to taste

3 quarts water

Instructions

Place all ingredients into a large stockpot and bring the water to a boil. Once boiling, skim any foam from the surface and lower the heat to maintain a steady simmer. Partially cover the pot and allow the broth to cook slowly for about three hours so the flavors can fully develop. Check occasionally to ensure it continues to simmer gently rather than boil rapidly.

When the broth is finished, remove and discard the solids using a slotted spoon. Strain the broth through a fine colander to create a smooth, clear liquid suitable for the clear liquid phase. Allow it to cool, then refrigerate until the fat rises and can be removed easily. Reheat the clear broth when ready to serve.

Mild Ginger Tea Broth

A soothing drink that may help calm nausea.

Ingredients

1 cup water

4 thin slices fresh ginger

½ teaspoon honey (optional)

Instructions

Place the ginger slices in a small pot with the water and bring to a gentle simmer. Allow the ginger to steep for about seven minutes so the flavor becomes warm and mild without becoming too strong. Once done, strain the liquid into a cup and discard the ginger slices. Sweeten lightly with honey if desired and sip while warm.

Light Vegetable Broth

A simple, strained broth with subtle flavor.

Ingredients

1 small carrot, chopped

1 small celery stick, chopped

½ small onion, chopped

4 cups water

Instructions

Place the vegetables and water in a small pot and bring to a gentle simmer. Cook for about twenty minutes, allowing the flavors to infuse the water. Once the broth is lightly fragrant, strain it thoroughly through a fine mesh sieve until the liquid is completely clear. Discard the vegetables and serve the clear broth warm.

Berry Infused Warm Water

A lightly flavored, refreshing drink that offers gentle hydration.

Ingredients

1 cup water, room temperature

2 or 3 blueberries or raspberries, lightly crushed

Fine mesh strainer

Instructions

Place the berries into a small cup or glass and press them gently with the back of a spoon to release a light amount of juice. Add the room temperature water and stir slowly to help the flavors blend without creating any strong or acidic notes. Allow the mixture to sit for a minute so the water absorbs a subtle hint of berry aroma and color while remaining clear and easy to digest.

Once the infusion has rested, strain the liquid through a fine mesh sieve to remove all berry solids. The result should be a lightly tinted, clear drink with a soft, refreshing flavor suitable for the clear liquid phase. Sip slowly to maintain hydration and enjoy a mild change from plain water without overwhelming the digestive system.

Lemongrass Tea Cup

Bright and calming with a delicate aroma.

Ingredients

1 lemongrass tea bag

1 cup hot water

Instructions

Place the lemongrass tea bag in a mug and pour hot water over it. Allow it to steep for five minutes so the light citrus aroma develops without becoming too strong.

Remove the tea bag and let the tea cool slightly until comfortable to sip. Drink slowly to support gentle hydration and calm digestion.

DINNER RECIPES

Beef Broth Variation

A deeper, savory flavor for evening comfort.

Ingredients

1 pound beef bones or lean beef pieces

1 small carrot, cut into chunks

1 small celery stalk

¼ onion

6 cups water

Salt to taste

Instructions

Place the beef bones or lean beef pieces into a medium pot along with the carrot, celery, and onion. Add the water and bring it slowly to a gentle boil so the flavors begin to release without creating too much richness. Once the broth reaches a boil, reduce the heat to a quiet simmer. Allow it to cook for about one hour, giving the vegetables and beef time to infuse the water and create a mild, comforting flavor that remains easy to digest.

When the broth has finished simmering, remove the pot from the heat and strain the liquid through a fine mesh sieve until it is completely clear. Discard all solids to keep the broth suitable for the clear liquid phase. Let the broth cool, then refrigerate it briefly so any fat rises to the surface and can be skimmed away easily. Reheat the broth gently before serving to enjoy a warm, soothing dinner that supports digestive rest.

Rooibos Tea Infusion

A smooth, caffeine free evening drink.

Ingredients

1 rooibos tea bag

1 cup hot water

Instructions

Place the rooibos tea bag in a mug and pour the hot water over it, allowing the tea to release its naturally warm, earthy flavor. Let it steep for about five minutes so the infusion becomes full and comforting without turning too strong. Rooibos naturally brews into a rich red color, but the liquid remains clear, making it suitable for the clear liquid phase.

Remove the tea bag and let the drink cool just slightly until it feels comfortable to sip. Rooibos is naturally caffeine free and gentle on digestion, making it a calming choice for evenings or moments when the stomach needs something mild. Sip slowly and allow its smooth flavor to offer steady hydration and warmth.

Mild Consommé Style Broth

A very refined, clear broth for sensitive digestion.

Ingredients

1 pound lean beef pieces or beef bones

1 small carrot, chopped

1 small celery stalk

¼ small onion

6 cups water

Small pinch of salt

Instructions

Place the beef, carrot, celery, onion, and water in a medium pot and bring to a gentle boil. Reduce the heat and let the mixture simmer quietly for about one hour until a light, mild broth forms. Keep the heat low so the broth stays clear and does not extract too much richness from the ingredients.

Strain the broth through a fine mesh sieve until the liquid is completely clear. Discard all solids. Chill the broth briefly so the fat rises to the surface and can be removed easily. Rewarm gently before serving.

Iced Herbal Lemon Tea

Comforting and easy for nighttime sipping.

Ingredients

4 herbal tea bags

3 green tea bags

3 tablespoons lemon juice

½ cup sugar, honey, or a light combination

6 cups water

Instructions

Bring the water to a gentle boil, then add the herbal tea bags and let them steep as the water cools slightly. This allows the herbal flavor to infuse the water without becoming too strong. When the water reaches a mild temperature of about 170 to 180 degrees, add the green tea bags and let them steep for just two minutes so the flavor remains smooth and light. Remove all of the tea bags as soon as the steeping time is over to keep the tea clear and easy to digest.

Stir in the lemon juice and your choice of sweetener, mixing until everything dissolves evenly. Let the tea cool to room temperature before placing it in the refrigerator to chill. Once cold, pour into a glass and enjoy a refreshing drink that stays gentle on the stomach while offering a mild, soothing flavor. This iced version provides variety in the clear liquid phase and can be especially comforting in the evening.

Clear Mushroom Broth Bowl

Earthy but mild, perfect for a quiet evening.

Ingredients

1 cup sliced white mushrooms

4 cups water

Small pinch of salt (optional)

Instructions

Place the mushrooms and water in a small pot and bring to a gentle simmer. Let the mixture cook for about fifteen to twenty minutes so the mushrooms lightly infuse the water. Keep the heat low so the broth stays pale and mild. Once the flavor has developed, strain the broth thoroughly through a fine mesh sieve until completely clear. Discard the mushroom pieces and serve the clear broth warm.

SNACK RECIPES

Rose Water Gelatin

Light, fragrant, and easy on the stomach.

Ingredients

1 packet unflavored gelatin

1 cup water

1 teaspoon rose water

Instructions

Begin by heating the water until it is warm but not boiling. Sprinkle the gelatin over the surface and stir slowly until it dissolves completely, allowing the mixture to become smooth and clear. Once the gelatin has blended with the water, add the rose water and stir again so the floral aroma is evenly distributed without overpowering the delicate flavor.

Pour the liquid into a small dish or container and place it in the refrigerator. Allow it to chill until fully set, creating a light and gently scented dessert that is easy on the stomach during the clear liquid phase. When ready, cut into small squares or spoon out portions and serve cold for a soothing, simple treat.

Clear Raspberry Gelatin

Simple and refreshing for a small energy boost.

Ingredients

½ packet clear raspberry flavored gelatin

1 cup hot water

Instructions

Heat the water until it is comfortably hot, then pour it into a small bowl. Add the raspberry gelatin powder and stir slowly until the mixture becomes completely smooth and clear. Make sure no grains remain at the bottom of the bowl, as fully dissolving the gelatin helps it set evenly and creates a clean, delicate texture.

Once the mixture is well combined, pour it into a small dish or container and place it in the refrigerator. Allow it to chill until firm, creating a light, gently flavored treat that is easy to tolerate during the clear liquid phase. Serve cold and in small portions to enjoy a refreshing hint of sweetness that supports hydration and comfort.

Cucumber Mint Infused Water

Cooling hydration throughout the day.

Ingredients

1 cup cold or warm water

2 slices cucumber

1 mint leaf

Instructions

Place the cucumber slices and mint leaf into a small cup or glass, gently pressing them with the back of a spoon to release a light amount of flavor. Pour the water over the ingredients and stir slowly so the subtle cucumber and mint essence begins to infuse. Let the mixture sit for a few minutes until the flavor becomes soft and refreshing without becoming strong or overwhelming.

Once lightly infused, strain the water through a fine mesh sieve to remove all solids. The result should be a clear, cool drink with a faint hint of cucumber and mint, offering gentle hydration that remains easy on the stomach. Sip slowly throughout the day as a soothing, refreshing option during the clear liquid phase.

Cranberry Water Variation

A gentle, slightly tart option.

Ingredients

¼ cup clear cranberry juice

¾ cup warm water or room temperature water

Instructions

Pour the cranberry juice into a small cup or glass, then add the water and stir slowly until the color blends into a soft, diluted pink. Warming the water slightly helps the flavors meld more evenly, but room temperature works well if that feels more comfortable. Make sure the drink stays light and mild, as the goal is to provide gentle hydration without strong acidity.

Once combined, let it sit for a moment so the temperature settles and the flavors soften. The finished drink should taste mildly tart and refreshing while remaining easy to tolerate during the clear liquid phase. Sip slowly to support hydration and comfort throughout the day.

Orange Blossom Warm Water

Lightly floral with a calming aroma.

Ingredients

1 cup warm water

½ teaspoon orange blossom water

Instructions

Warm the water until it reaches a comfortable sipping temperature, then pour it into a small cup or mug. Add the orange blossom water and stir slowly so the floral essence spreads evenly through the drink. The aroma should be soft and delicate rather than strong, creating a calming effect as the flavors settle into the warm liquid.

Let the mixture rest for a moment, allowing the heat to gently lift the scent of the orange blossoms. Sip it slowly while still warm so the mild floral notes remain soothing and light. This gentle drink offers a peaceful way to stay hydrated during the clear liquid phase and can be especially comforting in moments of bloating or tension.

CHAPTER 3

PHASE 2: LOW FIBER RECOVERY RECIPES

After the clear liquid stage has helped calm inflammation, the digestive system is ready for gentle, low fiber foods. This phase serves as a bridge between bowel rest and regular eating. Soft textures, mild flavors, and easily digested foods help the colon continue healing without strain. This period is essential for easing the digestive tract back to normal function while preventing discomfort or a return of symptoms.

The goal of this stage is to offer nourishment without overwhelming the intestines. Foods should be smooth, soft, and low in residue. Most vegetables should be well cooked, fruits should be peeled or blended into smooth textures, and proteins should be tender and simple. Eating slowly, chewing thoroughly, and spreading meals throughout the day can help maintain comfort as the body transitions from liquids to solids.

Below are supportive recipes for breakfasts, lunches, dinners, and snacks that fit comfortably into this stage of recovery.

BREAKFAST RECIPES

Soft Scrambled Eggs on White Toast

Creamy eggs paired with tender toast make a mild, balanced breakfast.

Ingredients

2 eggs

1 tablespoon milk

1 teaspoon butter

1 slice white bread

Instructions

Crack the eggs into a small bowl, add the milk, and whisk until the mixture becomes smooth and lightly foamy. Warm the butter in a nonstick pan over low heat, letting it melt slowly without browning. Pour in the egg mixture and cook gently, stirring slowly and continuously so the eggs thicken into soft, delicate curds. Keeping the heat low helps maintain a creamy texture that is easy to digest.

While the eggs finish cooking, lightly toast the slice of white bread until just warm and soft, not crisp. Spoon the creamy scrambled eggs over the toast while still warm. The soft texture and mild flavor make this breakfast gentle on the stomach during the low fiber recovery phase, offering protein and comfort without heaviness.

Baked Eggs With Mashed Potatoes

A warm, filling option that stays gentle on the stomach.

Ingredients

1 egg

½ cup prepared mashed potatoes

Pinch of salt

Instructions

Spoon the mashed potatoes into a small oven safe dish and spread them into an even layer. Make a shallow indentation in the center so the egg has a place to sit without spilling over. Crack the egg gently into the center of the potatoes and sprinkle a small pinch of salt on top. This keeps the flavors mild while allowing the potatoes to support the egg as it bakes.

Place the dish into a preheated 350°F oven and bake until the egg white is fully set and the yolk reaches your preferred level of firmness. The heat warms the potatoes through, creating a soft, comforting texture that pairs well with the gentle flavor of the baked egg. Serve warm for a simple dish that remains easy to digest during the low fiber recovery phase.

Soft Pancakes With Light Syrup

Mild, fluffy pancakes that go down easily.

Ingredients

Prepared pancake batter

Small drizzle of syrup

Instructions

Heat a nonstick pan over low to medium heat so the pancakes cook gently without browning too deeply. Spoon a small amount of batter into the pan and let it spread into a soft round shape. Cook slowly until tiny bubbles appear on the surface and the edges look slightly set, then flip carefully. Allow the second side to cook just until lightly golden, keeping the texture soft and tender rather than crisp.

Transfer the pancakes to a plate while still warm and drizzle a very small amount of syrup over the top. The sweetness should stay mild to keep the meal easy on digestion. These pancakes offer a soft, comforting option during the low fiber recovery phase, giving a feeling of warmth and fullness without heaviness.

Rice Cereal With Warm Milk

A classic low fiber breakfast for sensitive digestion.

Ingredients

½ cup rice cereal

1 cup warm milk

Instructions

Combine cereal and warmed milk. Stir until smooth and serve.

Strawberry Milk Smoothie (Strained)

A mild drink that adds variety while remaining gentle.

Ingredients

½ cup milk

2 tablespoons strawberry purée (strained)

Instructions

Combine the milk and the strained strawberry purée in a small blender or cup and blend briefly until the mixture looks smooth and pale pink. Keeping the blending time short helps prevent excess froth while still creating a uniform texture. If the strawberries leave any tiny seeds or pulp behind, pour the mixture through a fine mesh strainer to maintain a silky consistency that remains gentle on digestion.

Once blended and strained, let the smoothie sit for a moment so any remaining bubbles settle. Serve it chilled or at a cool room temperature, depending on what feels most comfortable. The soft flavor and smooth texture make this an easy way to introduce a little variety in the low fiber recovery phase while still keeping the stomach calm.

Mild Rice Porridge

A soft, comforting bowl that is easy to digest.

Ingredients

½ cup cooked white rice

1 cup water or broth

Instructions

Combine the cooked rice with the water or broth in a small saucepan and bring it to a gentle simmer. Cook over low heat, stirring occasionally, until the rice begins to break down and soften even further. As it simmers, the grains will gradually absorb the liquid and start to thicken, creating a very gentle consistency that is ideal during recovery.

Continue cooking until the mixture becomes creamy and smooth, adding a little more water if needed to reach your preferred texture. Use the back of a spoon to lightly mash any remaining whole grains so the porridge stays easy to digest. Serve warm for a soothing, simple meal that brings comfort without heaviness.

Soft Banana and Apple Mash

A simple blend of mild fruits without skins or chunks.

Ingredients

½ banana

½ peeled apple

Instructions

Peel and chop the apple into small pieces, then steam it briefly until it becomes soft enough to mash easily. Transfer the warm apple pieces to a small bowl and add the banana. Use a fork or spoon to mash the two fruits together until they form a smooth, uniform consistency without any noticeable chunks. The combination should be soft and mild, with a naturally sweet flavor that remains gentle on the stomach.

If needed, mash a little longer or add a small splash of warm water to achieve an even smoother texture. Serve slightly warm for the most soothing effect, or let it cool to room temperature if that feels more comfortable. This soft fruit mash provides a gentle way to add variety and natural sweetness during the low fiber recovery phase.

Cooked Carrots With Vanilla Notes

Soft and slightly sweet for a gentle morning option.

Ingredients

1 carrot, chopped

1 cup water

Drop of vanilla

Instructions

Place the chopped carrot into a small saucepan with the water and bring it to a gentle simmer. Cook over low heat until the carrot becomes very soft and tender, easily breaking apart when pressed with a spoon. Drain any remaining water and transfer the warm carrot pieces to a small bowl. Add a tiny drop of vanilla while the carrots are still warm so the flavor blends smoothly without overpowering the natural sweetness.

Mash the carrots until they reach a soft, uniform consistency. If needed, add a small splash of warm water to make the texture smoother and easier to digest. Serve warm as a mild, lightly sweet dish that feels comforting in the low fiber recovery phase and provides a gentle start to the morning.

French Toast With Maple Syrup

Soft, lightly sweet breakfast that stays easy to digest.

Ingredients

1 slice soft white bread

1 egg

2 tablespoons milk

Pinch of cinnamon (optional, very small amount)

½ teaspoon butter or oil for the pan

1 to 2 teaspoons maple syrup

Instructions

In a shallow bowl, whisk the egg and milk together until smooth. If tolerated, add a very small pinch of cinnamon for gentle flavor. Dip the slice of bread into the mixture, allowing it to soak up the liquid on both sides without becoming soggy or falling apart.

Warm the butter or oil in a nonstick pan over low to medium heat. Cook the soaked bread for 2 to 3 minutes on each side until it is lightly golden and cooked through in the center. Serve immediately with a small drizzle of maple syrup on top, keeping the portion modest so the meal stays mild and easy on the stomach.

Boiled Egg With White Bread Toast

Simple protein paired with soft bread.

Ingredients

1 egg

1 slice soft white bread

Small pinch of salt and pepper (optional, very light)

Instructions

Place the egg in a small pot and cover with cold water. Bring to a gentle boil, then reduce the heat and simmer for 8 to 10 minutes, depending on whether you prefer a softer or firmer yolk. Remove the egg, cool slightly under running water, then peel carefully.

While the egg cooks, toast the white bread very lightly so it remains soft rather than crisp. Slice the egg and place it on top of the toast, or serve them side by side. Sprinkle with a very light pinch of salt and pepper if tolerated. Enjoy warm for a mild, easy breakfast that offers protein without heaviness.

Pear Compote

Soft, spoonable fruit with a light sweetness.

Ingredients

1 ripe pear, peeled, cored, and chopped

2 tablespoons water

½ to 1 teaspoon sugar or honey

Tiny pinch of cinnamon or vanilla (optional)

Instructions

Place the chopped pear and water in a small saucepan over low heat. Cover and cook for 8 to 10 minutes, stirring occasionally, until the pear becomes very soft and begins to break down. If needed, add a teaspoon of extra water to prevent sticking.

Stir in the sugar or honey and, if tolerated, a tiny pinch of cinnamon or a drop of vanilla. Continue cooking for another minute until the compote is smooth and glossy. Mash lightly with a fork for a soft, chunky texture or blend briefly for a smoother finish. Serve warm or cooled as a gentle side or snack.

Apple Puree With Vanilla

Silky fruit puree with a gentle flavor.

Ingredients

1 soft apple, peeled, cored, and chopped

2 tablespoons water

½ to 1 teaspoon sugar or honey (optional)

⅛ teaspoon vanilla extract

Instructions

Place the peeled, cored, and chopped apple pieces into a small saucepan along with the water. Cover the pan and cook over very low heat for about 10 minutes, stirring occasionally to prevent sticking. As the apples soften, they will begin to break down on their own. If the mixture becomes too dry at any point, add a teaspoon of extra water to maintain moisture and ensure the apples cook evenly without browning or scorching. The goal is to keep the heat gentle so the fruit stays soft and mild in flavor.

Once the apples are extremely tender and easily mashed with a spoon, remove the pan from the heat. Stir in the vanilla extract and, if desired, the sugar or honey for a touch of sweetness. Mash the apples thoroughly with a fork for a soft, slightly textured puree, or blend briefly with an immersion blender for an ultra-smooth finish. Let the puree cool slightly before serving warm, or chill it for a cool, soothing snack. The final texture should be silky and completely free of skins or firm chunks, making it ideal for Phase 3 digestion.

LUNCH RECIPES

Grilled Chicken Sandwich on Soft Bread

Lightly seasoned chicken placed on soft white bread.

1 small boneless, skinless chicken breast or thigh

1 teaspoon olive oil

Pinch of salt

1 to 2 teaspoons water (for softening after cooking)

2 slices soft white bread

Instructions

Brush the chicken lightly with olive oil and sprinkle only a small pinch of salt on both sides. Heat a nonstick pan or grill pan over low to medium heat. Cook the chicken slowly for several minutes on each side until fully cooked through and pale in color. Avoid browning or creating grill marks so the texture stays soft and gentle for digestion. Once cooked, transfer the chicken to a cutting board and let it rest for a minute. Slice it into very thin, tender pieces so it is easy to chew. If the chicken feels slightly firm, place the slices back into the warm pan with a teaspoon or two of water and let them steam gently for a minute until softened.

Lay the thin chicken slices between the two pieces of soft white bread, pressing lightly so the sandwich holds together without becoming heavy. Serve the sandwich warm to keep the bread tender and the chicken moist. Cutting it into small squares or thin strips can make it even gentler to eat during the low fiber recovery phase.

Baked Fish With Mashed Potatoes

A classic meal that offers protein without heaviness.

Ingredients

1 small white fish fillet such as cod, haddock, tilapia, or pollock

½ cup mashed potatoes

2 to 3 tablespoons chicken or vegetable broth

Pinch of salt (optional)

Instructions

Preheat the oven to 350°F. Place the fish fillet in a small oven safe dish and pour the broth around the edges so the liquid sits at the bottom of the dish without covering the fish. This helps the fillet steam gently instead of drying out. If you prefer, sprinkle a tiny pinch of salt on top, keeping the seasoning very light. Cover the dish tightly with foil so the steam stays inside. Bake for about fifteen minutes, then check the texture. The fish is ready when it looks pale, moist, and flakes easily with a fork without forming a crust. If it still feels firm, cover again and bake for a few more minutes until tender.

Warm the mashed potatoes until smooth and soft. Transfer the baked fish to a plate and spoon a little of the warm broth from the baking dish over the top to keep it moist. Serve with the mashed potatoes for a mild, comforting meal that is gentle on digestion and easy to tolerate during the low fiber recovery phase.

Penne With Light Cheese Sauce

Smooth and creamy without overwhelming the stomach.

Ingredients

1 cup cooked penne

2 tablespoons mild cheese sauce

Instructions

Use penne that has been cooked until very soft, slightly beyond al dente, so it is easy to chew and gentle on digestion. Warm the mild cheese sauce in a small pan over low heat until it becomes smooth and slightly loosened. Add a teaspoon of warm water or milk if the sauce feels too thick. Gently stir the cooked penne into the warm cheese sauce, coating the pasta without creating a heavy or rich texture.

Allow the mixture to heat through briefly, just until warm and cohesive. Avoid simmering so the sauce stays mild and the pasta remains soft. Serve the dish warm for a simple, comforting meal that provides flavor without overstimulating the stomach during the low fiber recovery phase.

White Bread Sandwich With Cottage Cheese Spread

A mild, protein rich option that stays soft and easy on the stomach.

Ingredients

2 slices soft white bread

2 to 3 tablespoons cottage cheese, smooth or lightly mashed

Pinch of salt (optional)

Instructions

Spoon the cottage cheese into a small bowl and mash it lightly with a fork until the texture becomes soft and uniform. This makes the spread smoother and easier to tolerate during recovery. Add a small pinch of salt if needed, keeping the seasoning very light. Spread the cottage cheese gently over one slice of white bread, keeping the layer thin so the sandwich stays mild and soft.

Place the second slice of bread on top and press lightly so the sandwich holds together without becoming dense. Cut the sandwich into small squares or narrow strips for easier chewing. Serve fresh to maintain the soft texture that supports gentle digestion in the low fiber recovery phase.

Soft Scrambled Egg Rice Bowl

A warm, gentle meal that provides balanced protein and comfort.

Ingredients

1 whole egg

½ cup warm cooked white rice

1 teaspoon water or milk (optional, for softer texture)

Pinch of salt (optional)

Instructions

Crack the egg into a small bowl and whisk gently until the yolk and white combine. Add a teaspoon of water or milk if you prefer a softer, fluffier texture. Warm a nonstick pan over low heat and pour in the mixture. Stir slowly and continuously as the egg cooks, keeping the heat low so the curds form very gradually. Stop cooking while the eggs are still soft, moist, and pale yellow with no browning.

Spoon the warm white rice into a small bowl and spread it lightly. Place the soft scrambled egg on top, letting the warmth of the rice and egg blend together. Serve immediately for a mild, soothing meal that is easy to digest and comforting during the low fiber recovery phase.

Pasta With Butter and Parmesan

Simple and soothing.

Ingredients

1 cup cooked pasta

1 teaspoon butter

1 teaspoon grated Parmesan

Instructions

Use pasta that has been cooked until very soft so it remains easy to chew and gentle on the stomach. While the pasta is still warm, add the butter and stir slowly until it melts and coats each piece lightly. The goal is to keep the dish mild, so avoid browning the butter or adding any strong seasonings. Sprinkle the grated Parmesan over the warm pasta and stir again so the cheese melts gently into the butter, forming a thin, smooth coating.

Let the pasta sit for a moment so the flavors soften and the texture becomes cohesive. Serve warm for a simple, comforting meal that offers gentle flavor without heaviness, ideal for the low fiber recovery phase.

Chicken Broth With Carrot Shreds

Adds a tiny bit of fullness while still remaining low fiber.

Ingredients

1 cup chicken broth

1 tablespoon very finely grated cooked carrot

Instructions

Warm the chicken broth gently on the stovetop until steaming but not boiling. Add the finely grated, already cooked carrot just before serving and stir lightly so it disperses through the broth without sinking.

Chicken Noodle Soup Variation

A simplified, gentle version of a comforting classic.

Ingredients

1 cup chicken broth

Small handful soft noodles (about 2 to 3 tablespoons uncooked)

Instructions

Bring the chicken broth to a gentle simmer, then add the noodles. Cook them directly in the broth until they are completely soft and easy to chew, usually 8 to 10 minutes depending on noodle thickness. Serve warm once the noodles have absorbed some broth and reached a tender, delicate texture.

Baked Salmon With Boiled Potatoes

Soft, mild, and flaky.

Ingredients

1 small piece salmon (skin removed)

½ cup peeled, chopped potatoes

1 to 2 teaspoons broth or water (for baking)

Pinch of salt (optional)

Instructions

Place the salmon in a small oven safe dish and add one to two teaspoons of broth or water around it to keep it moist. Sprinkle a tiny pinch of salt if desired, but avoid strong spices or oil so the flavor remains mild. Cover the dish tightly with foil. Bake at 350°F for about 12 to 15 minutes, checking the texture at the 12-minute mark. The salmon is ready when it becomes pale in color, soft throughout, and flakes easily with almost no pressure. It should not brown, crisp, or firm up.

For the potatoes, peel and chop them into small pieces and boil in plain water until very soft, usually 12 to 15 minutes depending on size. The ideal texture is when a fork slides through effortlessly and the potato begins to break apart on its own. Drain and keep warm. Serve the tender salmon alongside the soft potatoes for a gentle, easy to digest meal.

Ricotta Rice Blend

Warm rice gently folded with ricotta for a soft, creamy texture.

Ingredients

½ cup warm cooked white rice

1 to 2 tablespoons ricotta cheese

Small pinch of salt (optional)

Instructions

Warm the cooked white rice until it is soft and slightly steamy. Spoon the ricotta into a small bowl and stir it gently to loosen the texture so it blends more easily. Add the ricotta to the warm rice and fold it in slowly until the mixture becomes creamy and cohesive. Keep the ratio light so the dish stays mild and easy to tolerate. Add a tiny pinch of salt if needed, keeping flavors very gentle.

Let the mixture rest for a moment so the warmth softens the ricotta even more. Serve immediately while warm for a smooth, comforting dish that provides a soft texture and mild flavor suitable for the low fiber recovery phase.

Tuna Salad With Light Mayo

Simple protein option.

Ingredients

2 tablespoons tuna drained well

1 teaspoon light mayo

Soft white bread (optional)

Instructions

Place the drained tuna in a small bowl and break it apart with a fork until it becomes soft and finely flaked. Add the light mayo and mix slowly until the texture turns smooth and cohesive. Keep the mixture mild without any additional seasonings to ensure it stays gentle on the stomach. If the tuna feels a little dry, add a few extra drops of mayo or warm water to soften it further.

Serve the tuna salad on its own or spread a very thin layer onto soft white bread for an easy to chew option. Cut the bread into small squares if you choose to use it. Enjoy immediately so the texture stays soft and moist. This simple mixture provides a light protein choice that remains easy to digest during the low fiber recovery phase.

White Pasta Salad Variation

A mild dinner option for transitioning toward more texture.

Ingredients

1 cup cooked white pasta

1 teaspoon light dressing

Instructions

Cook the white pasta until it is very soft and tender, slightly overcooking it to ensure it's easy to chew and digest. Drain and let the pasta cool to room temperature or warm slightly. Add the light dressing, using only a small amount to keep the flavor mild and the dish gentle on the stomach. Gently mix the pasta and dressing until evenly coated, ensuring no strong seasoning or oily texture.

Serve the pasta either warm or at room temperature for a simple, comforting meal that provides a mild transition to more texture during the low fiber recovery phase. The pasta should remain soft and easy to eat without being heavy or greasy.

DINNER RECIPES

Oven-Baked Chicken With Soft White Rice

A mild, protein-rich dinner served warm and tender.

Ingredients

1 small chicken breast

½ teaspoon olive oil

Pinch salt + pinch dried oregano

½ cup cooked soft white rice

Instructions

Coat the chicken breast lightly with olive oil, a small pinch of salt, and a gentle sprinkle of dried oregano. Place it in a baking dish and bake at 375°F (190°C) for 18 to 22 minutes, or until the center is fully cooked and the meat feels tender when pressed. To keep the chicken extra moist, cover it loosely with foil during the final few minutes of cooking so the steam softens the texture and prevents dryness.

Once done, let the chicken rest briefly before slicing it into thin, easy-to-chew pieces. Serve the chicken over or beside warm, soft white rice, allowing any juices from the pan to naturally soak into the rice for added flavor. Keep the seasoning mild and the texture soft to ensure the meal remains gentle on digestion and suitable for Phase 3 recovery.

Slow-Stewed Beef With White Rice

A gentle, fall-apart beef dish served with soft grains.

Ingredients

½ cup lean stew beef

½ cup white rice

¼ cup broth

Pinch salt

Instructions

Place the small pieces of lean stew beef in a small pot and pour the broth over them, adding a pinch of salt and a very light sprinkle of thyme or parsley if tolerated. Cover the pot and simmer over very low heat for 45 to 60 minutes, stirring occasionally and adding a splash more broth if needed. The beef should reach a point where it is extremely soft, shredding easily with a fork and staying moist without any toughness.

Warm the cooked white rice until soft and fluffy, then spoon it into a shallow bowl. Gently place the tender stewed beef on top or beside the rice, drizzling a little of the warm broth over both to enhance moisture and flavor. Serve immediately while everything is warm and soft, creating a gentle, soothing dinner suitable for Phase 3 recovery.

Creamy Spinach With Mashed Potatoes

Soft greens blended into smooth, comforting potatoes.

Ingredients

½ cup cooked spinach

½ cup mashed potatoes

Pinch salt + 1 teaspoon olive oil

Instructions

Start by cooking the spinach until it is soft and tender. You can steam or simmer the spinach for about 3-4 minutes until it wilts down completely. Once cooked, drain any excess water, and then finely chop or blend the spinach to a smooth texture, ensuring there are no tough pieces remaining. This step ensures that the spinach blends seamlessly into the mashed potatoes.

Next, prepare the mashed potatoes by heating them gently in a pot or microwave until warm and creamy. If needed, add a little bit of warm milk or water to ensure the potatoes are soft and smooth. Once the potatoes are ready, stir in the finely chopped spinach, olive oil, and a pinch of salt. Mix well until the spinach is evenly distributed throughout the mashed potatoes. The result should be a creamy, velvety texture with no firm pieces. Serve immediately while warm for a comforting, easy-to-digest meal.

Soft Turkey Meatloaf With Boiled Potatoes

Comfort food in a gentle, easy-to-digest form.

Ingredients

Slice of soft baked meatloaf (turkey or lean beef)

½ cup boiled potatoes

Pinch salt

Instructions

Warm the cooked meatloaf gently in the oven or microwave until soft. While the meatloaf is warming, boil the potatoes in a pot of water for 10–12 minutes, or until they are easily mashable. Drain and mash the potatoes with a pinch of salt for flavor. Serve the warm meatloaf alongside the creamy mashed potatoes.

Soft-Cooked Ham With Creamy Green Beans

Tender ham paired with very soft vegetables.

Ingredients

2–3 slices soft cooked ham

½ cup cooked green beans

Pinch salt + tiny drizzle olive oil

Instructions

Warm the ham gently in a skillet or oven until it reaches a comfortable serving temperature, ensuring it remains tender. Meanwhile, cook the green beans in boiling water until they are extremely soft, about 10–12 minutes. Once soft, drain and mash the beans lightly, adding a drizzle of olive oil and a pinch of salt to enhance the flavor.

Serve the warm ham alongside the creamy, mashed green beans, creating a comforting, mild dish.

Soft Veggie-Tofu Stir Fry

A fully softened vegetable blend with tender tofu.

Ingredients

½ cup tofu cubes (soft, not firm)

½ cup soft, well-cooked vegetables (such as well-cooked zucchini, carrots, and spinach)

Pinch of salt

Tiny drizzle of olive oil

Instructions

Start by sautéing the tofu in a teaspoon of olive oil on low heat until it's soft and heated through. Ensure that the tofu remains soft to avoid any hard or chewy texture. In a separate pan, cook the vegetables until they are extremely soft, either by simmering or steaming them until they break down. Once the vegetables are fully cooked, combine them with the tofu and stir gently for 1-2 minutes until everything is well mixed. Season lightly with salt to taste.

Serve immediately for a gentle, mild meal that is easy on digestion, with tender vegetables and soft tofu. The key is ensuring the vegetables are cooked until they are soft enough to be easily digested.

Baked Cod with White Rice

A soft, mild, and easy-to-digest meal.

Ingredients:

1 small piece of cod fillet

½ cup cooked white rice

Pinch salt

½ teaspoon olive oil

¼ cup water (for baking)

Instructions:

Preheat the oven to 350°F (175°C) and lightly grease a small baking dish with olive oil. Place the cod fillet into the baking dish and lightly season it with a pinch of salt. Add the water around the fish to help it stay moist as it bakes, and then cover the dish with foil to ensure the fish remains tender. Bake for 15-20 minutes, or until the fish is cooked through and flakes easily with a fork. The cod should be soft, tender, and easy to break apart, which is perfect for Phase 2 recovery.

While the cod is baking, cook the white rice according to package instructions, making sure it becomes soft and fluffy. Once cooked, gently fluff the rice with a fork, keeping it light and airy. When the fish is ready, serve it over the cooked rice, spooning any cooking juices from the baking dish over the top for added moisture and flavor. This simple, comforting dish is ideal for soothing the digestive system during recovery, offering a balance of mild protein and easily digestible carbohydrates. Serve immediately while warm to enjoy a gentle, nourishing meal.

SNACK AND DESSERT RECIPES

Applesauce

Smooth, naturally sweet, and soothing.

Ingredients

½ cup plain unsweetened applesauce

Optional: tiny drop of vanilla or cinnamon

Instructions

Place the unsweetened applesauce into a small serving bowl and decide whether you prefer it slightly chilled or gently warmed. To warm it, heat the applesauce on the stovetop over low heat or microwave it for 10 to 15 seconds, just until it reaches a soft, comforting temperature without becoming hot. If you'd like to add flavor, sprinkle in only the tiniest pinch of cinnamon or a single drop of vanilla, mixing thoroughly so the flavor stays delicate and soothing rather than strong.

Before serving, stir the applesauce until it becomes silky and uniform in texture. Enjoy it slowly, one spoonful at a time, allowing the smooth consistency to settle comfortably in the stomach. This simple preparation keeps the applesauce mild, soft, and ideal for sensitive digestion during recovery.

Canned Peaches

Soft fruit with mild sweetness.

Ingredients

½ cup canned peaches, skinless, in juice (not syrup)

Instructions

Drain the peaches and slice them into smaller pieces if needed. Warm slightly if preferred to soften them further. The fruit should be tender enough to mash easily with a fork. Serve in a small bowl for a light, soothing snack.

Pudding Cups

Soft, smooth, and easy to digest, a gentle sweet treat perfect for Phase 2.

Ingredients

1 can (13.5 oz) light coconut milk

4 large egg yolks (room temperature)

5 tablespoons arrowroot starch

1 teaspoon vanilla paste (or vanilla extract)

A few drops vanilla stevia or 1–2 teaspoons sugar (optional)

Instructions

In a double boiler over medium heat, whisk a small splash of the coconut milk with the egg yolks and arrowroot starch until the mixture becomes silky and free of lumps. Gradually add the rest of the coconut milk while whisking. Continue heating for about 10–12 minutes, whisking more frequently as it warms. As soon as the mixture thickens into a pudding-like consistency, remove it from heat immediately to prevent curdling.

Whisk in the vanilla paste and stevia or sugar. Pour the mixture through a fine mesh strainer into a heat-safe bowl to ensure an ultra-smooth texture. Let it cool to room temperature, then spoon into 2–4 small serving cups. Cover and refrigerate for at least 4 hours or overnight until fully set. Serve chilled for a soft, soothing dessert that supports gentle digestion.

Carrot Muffins

Soft, moist, and mildly sweet.

Ingredients

1 ¾ cups all-purpose flour

1 ½ teaspoons baking powder

½ teaspoon cinnamon (reduced)

¼ teaspoon baking soda

¼ teaspoon salt

⅛ teaspoon ground ginger (very small amount)

Pinch of nutmeg (optional, very tiny)

2 cups finely grated carrots

⅓ cup melted coconut oil or light olive oil

½ cup maple syrup or honey

2 eggs

1 cup plain Greek yogurt (or lactose-free yogurt)

1 teaspoon vanilla extract

1 tablespoon turbinado sugar for topping (optional)

Instructions

Preheat your oven to 425°F. Prepare a muffin tin by lightly greasing or lining with paper cups. In a large bowl, whisk together the flour, baking powder, cinnamon, baking soda, salt, ginger, and nutmeg. Add the finely grated carrots and stir gently so they disperse evenly throughout the dry mixture. In a separate bowl, whisk the oil and maple syrup, then add the eggs, yogurt, and vanilla, mixing until smooth and creamy.

Pour the wet ingredients into the dry ingredients and stir just until the batter comes together, keeping it soft and slightly lumpy for a tender texture. Divide the batter among 12 muffin cups and sprinkle a touch of turbinado sugar on top if desired. Bake for 13 to 16 minutes until the tops are lightly golden and a toothpick comes out clean. Let them cool for a few minutes before serving so they stay soft and moist, ideal for Phase 3 recovery.

White Rice Cakes With Apple Sauce

Light and tender with soft fruit sweetness.

Ingredients

1 plain white rice cake

2 tablespoons applesauce

Instructions

Spread the applesauce in a thin layer over the rice cake so the texture becomes softer and easier to chew. Let it sit for 1–2 minutes to slightly moisten the cake. Eat slowly for a gentle Phase 2 treat.

White Bread Toast With Jelly

Gentle sweetness on soft toast.

Ingredients

1 slice soft white bread

1 teaspoon smooth jelly (seedless)

Instructions

Toast the bread very lightly so it stays soft. Spread a thin layer of seedless jelly and cut into small squares for easier chewing. Serve immediately while warm and soft.

Lemon Sorbet

Cool, refreshing, and gentle.

Ingredients

½ cup water

1 tablespoon sugar or honey

1 tablespoon freshly squeezed lemon juice (strained to remove pulp and seeds)

Optional: 1–2 teaspoons additional water to adjust texture

Instructions

In a small saucepan, warm the water and sugar (or honey) over low heat until fully dissolved, creating a very light syrup. Remove from the heat and allow it to cool completely. Once cooled, stir in the strained lemon juice. The mixture should taste mildly sweet with just a soft hint of lemon so it remains gentle on the stomach.

Pour the mixture into a shallow freezer-safe dish and freeze for 1 to 2 hours. Every 20 to 30 minutes, scrape the mixture with a fork to break up any ice crystals and create a soft, slushy texture instead of a hard freeze. Once it reaches a smooth, icy consistency similar to a very soft sorbet, scoop out ½ cup. Let it sit at room temperature for 2 to 3 minutes to soften even more before serving so it stays easy to digest and not too cold.

Baked Oat Bites

Soft, warm, and lightly sweet.

Ingredients

½ cup cooked oats (very soft)

1 teaspoon honey

Optional: tiny pinch cinnamon (very light)

Optional: 1–2 teaspoons warm water to adjust softness

Instructions

In a small bowl, combine the warm cooked oats with honey, stirring slowly until the mixture becomes smooth, sticky, and uniform. If you choose to add cinnamon, use only the smallest pinch so the flavor stays gentle. If the oats seem too thick or firm, add a teaspoon or two of warm water to soften them until they can be shaped without resistance.

Line a small baking tray with parchment paper. Using a spoon, gently scoop the oat mixture into small soft mounds, shaping them lightly with the back of the spoon without pressing firmly. Place them on the tray and warm in the oven for about 5 minutes at very low heat (around 275°F / 135°C). The goal is only to slightly set the surface so they hold their shape while remaining soft and delicate inside. Remove from the oven and let cool briefly before serving warm.

Angel Food Cake With Strawberry Compote

Light cake topped with soft fruit.

Ingredients

For the Phase-2-Friendly Angel Food Cake (small batch)

½ cup egg whites (from about 4 large eggs)

¼ cup white sugar

¼ cup cake flour (or sifted all-purpose flour)

¼ teaspoon cream of tartar

½ teaspoon vanilla extract

Pinch of salt

For the Soft Strawberry Compote

½ cup chopped strawberries (fresh or thawed frozen)

1 to 2 teaspoons water

½ to 1 teaspoon sugar or honey (optional)

Instructions

1. Make the Soft Angel Food Cake

Preheat your oven to 325°F (165°C). Line a very small loaf pan or mini-cake pan with parchment paper. In a clean bowl, beat the egg whites with cream of tartar and a pinch of salt until soft peaks form. Slowly add the sugar while continuing to beat until the mixture becomes thick, glossy, and forms stiff peaks. Gently sift the flour over the top and fold it in using slow, sweeping motions to avoid deflating the batter. Add the vanilla and fold once more until fully blended.

Pour the batter into the prepared pan and smooth the top. Bake for 20 to 25 minutes until the cake is lightly golden and springs back when touched. Let it cool in the pan, then remove and set aside. The cake should be soft, sponge-like, airy, and very easy to chew, making it safe for Phase 2 when eaten in small portions.

2. Make the Strawberry Compote

Place the chopped strawberries and water in a small saucepan over low heat. Allow them to simmer gently for 6 to 8 minutes, stirring occasionally until the berries break down completely and form a soft, spoonable mixture. If you prefer extra sweetness, add a tiny amount of sugar or honey. Cook for another minute to blend the flavors, then remove from heat and mash lightly until smooth.

3. Assemble the Dessert

Warm 2 tablespoons of the compote so it becomes silky. Place a small slice of the soft angel food cake on a plate and gently spoon the warm compote over the top. Let it sit for a moment so the cake absorbs some moisture and becomes even softer. Serve immediately for a pleasant, mild, easy-to-digest Phase 2 dessert.

Honey-Glazed Baked Pears

Silky, warm, and lightly sweet.

Ingredients

1 ripe pear, peeled and sliced

1 teaspoon honey

1 tablespoon water

Instructions

Place the thin pear slices into a small baking dish in an even layer so they cook uniformly. Drizzle the honey over the pears, then add the tablespoon of water to the bottom of the dish to help create moisture and prevent sticking. Cover the dish tightly with foil to trap steam, ensuring the pears soften without browning or drying out.

Bake at 350°F (175°C) for about 15 to 20 minutes, checking once after 15 minutes. The pear should be extremely soft, almost spoon-tender, with the juices forming a light honey glaze in the dish. Remove from the oven and gently spoon the warm glaze over the pears before serving. Enjoy while warm for a soothing, easily digestible Phase 2 dessert.

CHAPTER 4

PHASE 3: HIGH FIBER DIET RECIPES

Once the digestive system has fully recovered from a flare and low fiber foods are tolerated comfortably, the body is ready to transition into a high fiber eating pattern. This stage plays an important role in long term management, as fiber helps soften stool, supports smoother bowel movements, and reduces pressure inside the colon. A steady high fiber routine can make flare ups less likely and support overall colon health.

Introducing fiber should be done gradually. Increasing intake too quickly may lead to bloating or gas, so allowing the intestine time to adjust is essential. Cooked vegetables, whole grains, fruits without skins, and plant based proteins can be excellent ways to build up fiber intake without overwhelming the digestive system. Hydration is equally important, as water helps fiber function effectively within the body.

Below are supportive, gentle recipes that offer the benefits of fiber without overly complex textures or ingredients. Each dish is designed to help you ease into this phase with comfort and confidence.

BREAKFAST RECIPES

Whole Grain Toast With Avocado Mash

Soft, creamy avocado on warm whole grain toast.

Ingredients

1 slice whole grain bread

¼ ripe avocado

Pinch of salt

Instructions

Toast the whole grain bread lightly until just warm and soft, avoiding crisping it too much so the texture stays gentle on the stomach. While the bread is toasting, peel and mash the ripe avocado with a fork until smooth and creamy, leaving no lumps. If needed, add a tiny pinch of salt to enhance the flavor, but keep it minimal for mildness. Once the toast is warm, spread the mashed avocado evenly over the top, ensuring the toast remains soft.

Serve immediately while warm for a simple, creamy dish that combines soft textures with the gentle nourishment of avocado. This makes a mild, easy-to-digest meal during the low fiber recovery phase, offering healthy fats without overwhelming the stomach.

Warm Oatmeal With Mixed Berries

A soothing, fiber rich bowl for the morning.

Ingredients

½ cup oats

1 cup water or milk

¼ cup soft berries(such as blueberries, raspberries, or strawberries)

Instructions

Place the oats and water or milk in a small saucepan and bring to a gentle simmer over low heat. Stir occasionally and cook until the oats are very soft and tender, about 10-15 minutes. If needed, add a little more water or milk during cooking to keep the oatmeal creamy. Once the oats are tender and have absorbed most of the liquid, add the soft berries and stir gently. Let the mixture simmer for a few more minutes until the berries begin to soften and release their juices, creating a slight berry flavor throughout the oatmeal.

Serve the warm oatmeal immediately, making sure the texture is creamy and smooth. This mild, fiber-rich meal is perfect for a gentle, nourishing start to the day, providing easy digestion and soft, soothing flavors.

Raisin Bran Muffins Variation

A gentle way to add more fiber to your day.

Ingredients

1 ½ cups white flour (or a 50:50 blend of white and whole wheat flour)

1 teaspoon baking powder

½ teaspoon baking soda

Pinch of salt

1 teaspoon ground cinnamon (optional, very small amount)

1 egg (or 1 tablespoon applesauce as a substitute)

2 tablespoons honey (or maple syrup)

2 tablespoons vegetable oil (or melted butter)

1/3 cup unsweetened applesauce (or mashed banana)

½ cup unsweetened almond milk (or oat milk)

½ cup small raisins or optional dried fruit

1 teaspoon vanilla extract

Instructions

Preheat the oven to 350°F (175°C) and line a muffin tin with paper liners. In a medium bowl, combine the dry ingredients: flour, baking powder, baking soda, salt, and cinnamon. In a separate bowl, whisk together the wet ingredients: egg, honey, oil, applesauce, milk, and vanilla extract. Pour the wet ingredients into the dry ingredients and stir gently until just combined. Be careful not to overmix the batter, as this could affect the texture of the muffins.

Fold in the raisins or any other dried fruit of your choice, mixing them in lightly. Scoop the batter into the prepared muffin tin, filling each cup about 2/3 full. Bake for about 15-20 minutes, or until a toothpick inserted into the center of the muffins comes out clean. Allow the muffins to cool slightly before serving to maintain their soft, tender texture.

Quinoa Breakfast Bowl With Fruit

A protein rich base paired with soft, sweet fruit.

Ingredients

½ cup cooked quinoa

¼ cup soft fruit pieces (such as berries, banana slices, or soft peaches)

Instructions

Begin by cooking the quinoa according to package instructions until it is soft and fluffy, then allow it to cool slightly. Spoon the quinoa into a small bowl and add the soft fruit pieces on top. Gently mix the quinoa and fruit together, taking care not to mash the fruit too much. If you prefer, you can warm the quinoa slightly before adding the fruit to keep the dish soothing and mild.

Serve the quinoa bowl either warm or at room temperature for a light, protein-rich breakfast option. The quinoa should be soft and fluffy, while the fruit should be tender and sweet, providing a gentle combination for an easy-to-digest meal during the low fiber recovery phase.

Vegetable Omelet With Whole Grain Toast

Soft cooked vegetables folded into a fluffy omelet.

Ingredients

2 eggs

¼ cup cooked vegetables

1 slice whole grain toast

Instructions

Crack the eggs into a bowl and whisk gently until the mixture is smooth. Warm a nonstick pan over low heat and pour in the egg mixture, allowing it to cook slowly so it remains soft and fluffy. Add the cooked vegetables to one side of the omelet and gently fold the eggs over them once the bottom is set, allowing the omelet to cook through without becoming firm or dry.

While the omelet finishes cooking, toast the whole grain bread lightly, just enough to warm it without crisping it. Serve the soft vegetable omelet alongside the warm toast for a simple, mild meal.

Greek Yogurt With Fruit Mix

Creamy yogurt topped with soft, fiber rich fruit.

Ingredients

½ cup Greek yogurt

¼ cup cooked or soft fruit(such as berries, banana slices, or stewed apples)

Instructions

Spoon the Greek yogurt into a small bowl, ensuring it's smooth and creamy. Gently mix in the soft fruit or place it on top of the yogurt, depending on your preference. If using cooked or stewed fruit, make sure it is soft and tender to blend easily with the yogurt. If you like, you can lightly mash the fruit to make it even softer and easier to digest.

Serve immediately for a mild, fiber-rich snack or breakfast that offers protein and natural sweetness. The creamy texture of the yogurt pairs perfectly with the soft fruit, making this a gentle option for sensitive digestion.

Banana Nut Muffins Variation

A gentle, lightly textured breakfast option.

Ingredients:

2 cups white flour (or oat flour)

½ cup rolled oats (optional, can be omitted for an even gentler texture)

1 teaspoon ground cinnamon (optional)

1 teaspoon baking powder (skip baking soda)

½ teaspoon salt (optional)

1 ⅓ cups mashed banana (about 3 medium or 2 large ripe bananas)

2 large eggs

⅓ cup melted coconut oil (or vegetable oil or melted butter)

⅓ cup maple syrup (or a small amount of mild sweetener)

⅓ cup milk (any kind, unsweetened almond or oat milk is a great choice)

1 teaspoon pure vanilla extract

¼ cup finely chopped nuts (optional, use light nuts like walnuts)

Instructions

Preheat the oven to 350°F (177°C) and prepare a 12-count muffin pan by greasing it with nonstick spray or using cupcake liners. In a large bowl, combine the flour, oats (if using), cinnamon, baking powder, and salt. In a separate bowl, mash the ripe bananas until smooth, then add the eggs, oil, maple syrup, milk, and vanilla, whisking them together until fully combined.

Next, pour the wet ingredients into the dry ingredients and stir gently until just combined. Be careful not to overmix, as this can affect the texture. If using, fold in the finely chopped nuts until they are evenly distributed through the batter. Once the batter is ready, spoon it into the muffin tin, filling each liner to the top.

Bake the muffins for 5 minutes at 425°F (218°C), then reduce the oven temperature to 350°F (177°C) and continue baking for another 15-16 minutes, or until a toothpick inserted into the center of the muffins comes out clean. After baking, let the muffins cool for 5 minutes in the pan before transferring them to a wire rack to cool completely.

Chia Seed Pudding

Smooth, mild, and rich in soluble fiber.

Ingredients

2 tablespoons chia seeds

½ cup milk (any kind, unsweetened almond or oat milk is a great choice)

Touch of honey (optional)

¼ cup mashed or sliced soft fruit (such as berries, banana, or mango)

Instructions

In a small bowl, combine the chia seeds, milk, and honey (if using). Stir well to ensure the chia seeds are evenly distributed in the liquid. Cover the bowl and refrigerate for a few hours, or overnight, to allow the pudding to thicken and the chia seeds to absorb the liquid, creating a creamy texture.

Spinach and Mushroom Omelet

Soft vegetables mixed into a warm omelet.

Ingredients

2 eggs

¼ cup raw spinach, chopped

¼ cup raw mushrooms, sliced

Pinch of salt (optional)

1 teaspoon olive oil or butter (for sautéing)

Optional: pinch of mild seasoning like garlic powder or a tiny pinch of dried thyme

Instructions

In a nonstick pan, sauté the mushrooms in olive oil or butter over low to medium heat until soft, about 3-4 minutes. Add the chopped spinach and cook until wilted and tender, about 2-3 minutes. The vegetables should be soft and tender, without any crispness. If desired, season lightly with salt and mild spices like garlic powder or dried thyme.

Meanwhile, whisk the eggs and cook them in a separate pan over low heat until set but soft. Once the eggs are cooked, gently fold the sautéed spinach and mushrooms into the omelet. Serve immediately for a soft, easy-to-digest meal.

Whole Grain Pancakes With Berry Compote

Soft pancakes topped with warm fruit.

Ingredients

1 cup white flour or oat flour

¾ cup unsweetened almond milk

1 teaspoon cinnamon (optional or very small amount)

1 teaspoon baking powder

1 egg (or ¼ cup mashed banana or applesauce as a substitute)

¼ cup soft fresh berries (such as mashed strawberries or blueberries)

3 tablespoons maple syrup (optional or reduced amount)

Instructions

In a small bowl, combine the white flour or oat flour, baking powder, and cinnamon (if using). In a separate bowl or measuring cup, whisk together the almond milk and egg (or egg substitute). Add the wet ingredients to the dry ingredients, mixing gently until just combined, being careful not to overmix. Heat a nonstick skillet over medium heat and lightly grease it with olive oil. Scoop ¼ cup portions of batter onto the skillet and cook until the edges of the pancakes turn golden brown, about 2-3 minutes, then flip and cook for another 1-2 minutes.

While the pancakes are cooking, prepare the berry compote by placing the soft fresh berries (or cooked berries) and maple syrup in a small saucepan over low heat. Gently simmer until the berries soften and release their juices, creating a light compote. Once the pancakes are done, serve them warm, topped with the berry compote. Enjoy a gentle, soothing breakfast that is mild and easy to digest.

Breakfast Quinoa With Fresh Fruit

Warm, lightly sweet, and high in fiber.

Ingredients

½ cup cooked quinoa

2 tablespoons soft fruit(such as mashed banana, berries, or soft peaches)

Instructions

Warm the cooked quinoa gently in a small pan over low heat, adding a tiny splash of water or milk to keep it soft and moist. Stir occasionally to prevent it from drying out. Once the quinoa is warm, fold in the soft fruit of your choice, such as mashed banana, berries, or soft peach slices. Stir gently until the fruit is evenly distributed, allowing the sweetness and flavor to blend into the quinoa.

Serve the quinoa immediately, while it's still warm, for a light and nourishing breakfast option. The soft fruit will add natural sweetness and vibrant color, creating a comforting and easy-to-digest meal perfect for Phase 2 recovery.

Whole Grain Pancakes With Maple Syrup

A classic breakfast with added fiber.

Ingredients

1 cup whole grain pancake mix (or a blend of whole wheat flour and oats for gentler digestion)

¾ cup unsweetened almond milk (or any milk of choice)

1 egg

1 teaspoon baking powder

1 teaspoon vanilla extract (optional)

1 teaspoon maple syrup (for serving)

Instructions

In a mixing bowl, whisk together the whole grain pancake mix, baking powder, and a pinch of salt. In a separate bowl, combine the almond milk, egg, and vanilla extract, and whisk until fully mixed. Add the wet ingredients to the dry ingredients, stirring gently until just combined, avoid overmixing to keep the texture light and fluffy.

Preheat a nonstick skillet over medium-low heat and lightly grease it. Scoop ¼ cup portions of the pancake batter into the skillet and cook until bubbles appear on the surface, about 2-3 minutes. Flip the pancakes and cook for an additional 1-2 minutes until golden brown and cooked through. Serve the pancakes warm with a drizzle of maple syrup on top for a naturally sweet, mild breakfast.

Almond Butter Overnight Oats

Creamy, filling, and ideal for busy mornings.

Ingredients

½ cup oats

½ cup milk (any kind, unsweetened almond milk or oat milk works well)

1 teaspoon almond butter

Instructions

In a small bowl or jar, combine the oats, milk, and almond butter. Stir well until the almond butter is evenly incorporated into the milk and oats, creating a creamy mixture. Cover the bowl or jar with a lid or plastic wrap and refrigerate overnight to allow the oats to absorb the liquid and soften. In the morning, give the oats a good stir to make sure everything is well-mixed and creamy.

Serve immediately, and if you like, top with some fresh fruit or a small drizzle of honey for extra flavor. The oats should be soft, creamy, and easy to digest, perfect for a quick, nourishing breakfast to start your day.

High Fiber Breakfast Burrito

A warm, soft wrap filled with gentle, fiber rich ingredients.

Ingredients

1 soft whole grain tortilla

2 scrambled eggs (soft cooked)

2 tablespoons cooked black beans (soft, no skins if possible)

2 tablespoons cooked spinach (well softened)

1 tablespoon mashed avocado

Pinch of salt

Optional: tiny pinch of mild paprika or cumin (very light)

Instructions

Warm the soft whole grain tortilla in a pan over low heat until flexible. In another pan, scramble the eggs gently on low heat so they remain soft and moist rather than firm or rubbery. Combine the cooked black beans and soft spinach, warming them slightly and mashing the beans a little so the texture stays easy to digest. Add a pinch of salt and a very tiny sprinkle of mild paprika or cumin only if tolerated.

Spread the mashed avocado in a thin layer on the tortilla, then spoon the soft eggs and vegetable mixture onto the center. Roll the tortilla gently into a burrito, tucking in the sides so the filling stays contained. Serve warm for a fiber balanced meal that remains gentle on the stomach while supporting Phase 3 recovery.

Multi Seed Whole Grain Bread With Smashed Avocado

A hearty, soft slice topped with creamy, nourishing avocado.

Ingredients

1 slice soft multi seed whole grain bread (avoid overly crunchy or seeded crusts)

¼ to ½ ripe avocado

Pinch of salt

Optional: tiny squeeze lemon juice

Optional: pinch of mild herbs such as dried basil

Instructions

Toast the multi seed whole grain bread very lightly, just enough to warm it while keeping the texture soft and easy to chew. Scoop the ripe avocado into a small bowl and mash until completely smooth, adding a pinch of salt and a drop of lemon juice if tolerated for brightness. If you'd like more flavor, sprinkle the smallest amount of mild dried basil.

Spread the mashed avocado evenly over the warm bread, ensuring the avocado layer is smooth and gentle. Let the bread sit for one minute so the avocado softens it further. Serve immediately for a creamy, fiber friendly, Phase 3 appropriate breakfast.

LUNCH RECIPES

Grilled Vegetable and Quinoa Salad

Soft, warm vegetables paired with fluffy quinoa.

Ingredients

½ cup cooked quinoa

½ cup grilled vegetables(such as zucchini, bell peppers, and eggplant)

Instructions

Start by cooking the quinoa according to package instructions, ensuring it's soft and fluffy. While the quinoa is cooking, grill the vegetables of your choice: zucchini, bell peppers, and eggplant work well. Grill the vegetables until they are tender and soft with a slight char, ensuring they stay moist without becoming too dry or firm. Allow the vegetables to cool slightly before chopping them into bite-sized pieces.

Once the quinoa is cooked and the vegetables are ready, mix them together gently in a bowl, ensuring they're evenly distributed. Season lightly with a pinch of salt and optional mild herbs or olive oil to keep the flavors simple and gentle. Serve warm or at room temperature for a light, soothing meal that combines protein-rich quinoa with soft, flavorful vegetables.

Lentil Soup With Whole Grain Roll

Comforting and fiber rich.

Ingredients

1 cup cooked lentils

2 cups broth (vegetable or chicken broth works well)

Whole grain roll(soft)

Instructions

Combine the cooked lentils and broth in a medium pot and bring the mixture to a gentle simmer over low heat. Allow it to cook for 10 to 15 minutes so the lentils can soften further and the broth can develop a warm, blended flavor. Stir occasionally to keep the lentils from settling at the bottom and adjust the heat as needed to maintain a slow, steady simmer. The soup should become slightly thicker as it cooks, but remain smooth and easy to digest.

Once warmed through, ladle the soup into a bowl and pair it with a soft whole grain roll. You may warm the roll briefly in the oven or microwave to keep the texture tender and easy to chew. Serve immediately for a mild, comforting meal that offers fiber, warmth, and gentle nourishment during Phase 3 recovery.

Chickpea Salad Sandwich

Creamy chickpeas on whole grain bread.

Ingredients

⅓ cup raw chickpeas

1 teaspoon mild dressing (made from 1 teaspoon olive oil, 1 teaspoon lemon juice, and a small pinch of salt)

2 slices whole grain bread

Instructions

To prepare the chickpeas, boil dried chickpeas until they are tender and easy to mash, which typically takes about 45 minutes to 1 hour. If using canned chickpeas, simply drain and rinse them thoroughly before mashing. Once the chickpeas are tender and soft, mash them with a fork or potato masher until smooth but still slightly chunky for texture. You want a creamy yet slightly textured consistency that holds together well.

Once the chickpeas are mashed and the dressing is ready, mix them together until the chickpeas are evenly coated. Spread the chickpea mixture onto two slices of soft whole grain bread. Cut the sandwich into halves and serve immediately for a comforting, protein-rich meal.

Veggie Wrap With Hummus

A soft, flavorful wrap full of gentle fiber.

Ingredients

Whole grain wrap(soft, not too firm)

2 tablespoons hummus

¼ cup soft cooked vegetables(such as zucchini, bell peppers, or spinach)

Instructions

Begin by warming the whole grain wrap slightly to make it more pliable and easier to roll. Spread 2 tablespoons of hummus evenly over the center of the wrap, ensuring a smooth layer. Then, add the soft cooked vegetables, such as zucchini, bell peppers, or spinach on top of the hummus, making sure they are tender and easy to digest.

Carefully fold the sides of the wrap inwards, then roll it tightly from the bottom up, enclosing the filling securely. Slice the wrap in half, if desired, and serve immediately for a soft, nutritious meal that combines healthy fats, fiber, and gentle vegetables.

Turkey and Avocado Wrap

Lean protein paired with creamy fiber.

Ingredients

Sliced turkey

Mashed avocado

Whole grain wrap

Instructions

Start by warming the whole grain wrap slightly to make it more pliable and easier to roll. Spread a generous amount of mashed avocado over the center of the wrap, ensuring it's smooth and evenly distributed. Layer the thinly sliced turkey on top of the avocado, making sure the slices are tender and not too thick for easy digestion.

Carefully fold in the sides of the wrap, then roll it tightly from the bottom up, ensuring the ingredients are secure. Slice the wrap in half, if desired, and serve immediately.

Chickpea and Quinoa Salad

Light yet filling.

Ingredients

A light, nourishing salad with quinoa, chickpeas, and fresh vegetables.

Ingredients

1 cup uncooked quinoa, rinsed

2 cups water

1 can (15 ounces) chickpeas, drained and rinsed

1 medium cucumber, chopped

1 medium red bell pepper, chopped

¾ cup red onion, chopped

1 cup flat-leaf parsley, chopped

¼ cup olive oil

¼ cup lemon juice (from 2-3 lemons)

1 tablespoon red wine vinegar

2 cloves garlic, minced

½ teaspoon fine sea salt

Freshly ground black pepper, to taste

Instructions

In a saucepan, combine the rinsed quinoa and water. Bring to a boil, then reduce heat to a simmer and cook until quinoa absorbs the water (about 15 minutes). Remove from heat and let it rest, covered, for 5 minutes.

In a large bowl, combine the cooked quinoa, chickpeas, cucumber, bell pepper, onion, and parsley. In a small bowl, whisk together olive oil, lemon juice, vinegar, garlic, salt, and pepper. Pour the dressing over the salad and toss gently.

Let the salad rest for 5-10 minutes before serving to allow the flavors to meld. Serve chilled or at room temperature.

Vegetable Lemon Vinaigrette Bowl

A refreshing, soft vegetable salad.

Ingredients

½ cup cooked vegetables

Splash lemon vinaigrette (made from lemon juice, olive oil, and a pinch of salt)

Instructions

In a bowl, combine the cooked vegetables with a splash of lemon vinaigrette. Gently toss the vegetables to ensure they are evenly coated in the dressing. If desired, you can let the salad sit for a few minutes to allow the flavors to meld. Serve immediately as a light, refreshing dish, perfect for a Phase 3 recovery meal that's both mild and nourishing.

Heartwarming Tomato and Lentil Soup

Smooth and hearty.

Ingredients

1 cup cooked lentils

1 cup tomato broth

Instructions

In a medium pot, combine the cooked lentils and tomato broth. Bring the mixture to a gentle simmer over low heat, stirring occasionally to ensure the lentils are evenly heated. Allow it to simmer for about 5–10 minutes until the soup is thoroughly warmed and the flavors are blended.

Once the soup is heated through, serve it immediately for a warm, nourishing meal. The lentils should be tender and the soup smooth, offering a comforting and fiber-rich option perfect for Phase 3 recovery.

Corn and Spinach Salad Cup

Soft textures with mild flavor.

Ingredients

¼ cup cooked corn

¼ cup cooked spinach

Instructions

In a small bowl, combine the cooked corn and cooked spinach, mixing gently to ensure the ingredients are evenly distributed. The vegetables should be tender and soft, allowing for easy digestion. If necessary, you can warm the mixture slightly to maintain a soothing, comfortable temperature.

Season lightly with a pinch of salt and a small drizzle of olive oil, if desired, to enhance the flavors without overpowering the softness of the vegetables. Serve immediately in a small cup or bowl for a light, mild meal that is easy to digest and full of gentle nutrition for Phase 3 recovery.

Wholemeal Pasta Salad Bowl

Gentle and nourishing with soft vegetables and a mild dressing.

Ingredients

1 lb whole wheat rotini pasta, cooked & drained

1 cup cooked baby carrots, chopped (substitute for raw bell pepper)

1 ½ cups cooked spinach or steamed arugula (substitute for raw arugula)

1/2 cup cooked zucchini or yellow squash, thinly sliced (substitute for raw red onion)

1/3 cup ricotta cheese (substitute for feta, for a milder option)

For the Lemon Vinaigrette

½ cup extra virgin olive oil

1 ½ teaspoons honey (adjust to taste)

2 tablespoons lemon juice

Pinch of salt (optional)

Instructions

Start by cooking the pasta according to package instructions, then drain and rinse it gently under warm water to keep it soft and easy to digest. For the vegetables, lightly steam the baby carrots and zucchini or yellow squash until tender. Sauté the spinach or arugula until just wilted for a softer texture. Allow the vegetables to cool slightly before combining them with the pasta.

To make the dressing, whisk together the olive oil, honey, and lemon juice until smooth and well combined. If you prefer a mild flavor, add just a pinch of salt. In a large bowl, combine the pasta, cooked vegetables, and ricotta cheese. Drizzle the dressing over the salad and toss gently until everything is well-coated. Serve immediately while still warm, or chill in the fridge for a few hours to let the flavors meld together.

Soft Grilled Portobello Mushroom Sandwich

A tender mushroom "burger" with gentle flavor and easy chewing.

Ingredients

1 soft whole grain bun or bread slice (lightly warmed)

1 large portobello mushroom cap

1 teaspoon olive oil

Pinch salt

Pinch dried oregano

Optional: 1 teaspoon mashed avocado for spread

Instructions

Brush the mushroom cap with olive oil and sprinkle lightly with salt and oregano. Cook it in a pan or grill pan over low to medium heat for 5 to 7 minutes per side until extremely soft and juicy, with no firm or rubbery texture remaining.

Warm the whole grain bun lightly so it stays soft. Spread a thin layer of mashed avocado if using, then place the mushroom on top. Press gently and serve warm for a mild, tender Phase 3 lunch that mimics a veggie burger without harsh textures.

Butternut Squash and Soft Lentil Comfort Soup

A warm, blended bowl rich in fiber yet gentle on the stomach.

Ingredients

½ cup cooked red or yellow lentils

½ cup cooked butternut squash cubes

1 ½ cups vegetable broth

Pinch salt

Optional: tiny pinch of turmeric or cumin (very light)

Instructions

Add the cooked lentils and butternut squash to a pot with the vegetable broth. Simmer over low heat for 10 minutes, stirring occasionally as the vegetables break down. If using spices, add only a tiny pinch to keep the flavor mild.

Mash the soup lightly with a spoon for texture or blend it partially for a creamier consistency. Warm until smooth and soft, then serve immediately for a soothing, Phase 3–safe lunch.

Three Bean Salad With Olive Oil Dressing

A soft, protein rich bean mix lightly dressed for gentle digestion.

Ingredients

¼ cup cooked kidney beans (soft, no firm skins)

¼ cup cooked chickpeas (very soft, skins removed if needed)

¼ cup cooked cannellini or black beans (soft)

2 tablespoons finely diced soft vegetables (cooked zucchini or carrot)

1 teaspoon olive oil

1 teaspoon lemon juice

Small pinch salt

Optional mild herbs: dried basil or parsley (very light)

Instructions

Combine the three types of cooked beans in a small bowl, ensuring all of them are tender enough to mash easily with a fork. Add the finely diced soft vegetables and gently fold the mixture so the beans stay intact but well blended.

In a separate small bowl, whisk together the olive oil, lemon juice, salt, and a tiny pinch of dried basil or parsley if you want a mild flavor. Pour this dressing over the bean mixture and toss lightly until evenly coated. Serve at room temperature for a soft, satisfying Phase 3 lunch that offers gentle fiber without irritating the digestive system.

DINNER RECIPES

Baked Fish With Vegetables

A simple, high fiber dinner.

Ingredients

1 small fish fillet(such as tilapia, cod, or salmon)

½ cup cooked vegetables (such as carrots, zucchini, or spinach)

Instructions

Preheat the oven to 375°F (190°C). Place the fish fillet on a baking sheet lined with parchment paper or lightly greased. Season with a pinch of salt and a drizzle of olive oil. Bake for 10-15 minutes, or until the fish flakes easily with a fork and becomes tender. While the fish is baking, cook the vegetables until they are soft and easily mashable. You can steam or sauté the vegetables, depending on your preference.

Once the fish is done, remove it from the oven and serve it alongside the soft, cooked vegetables. Ensure the fish is tender and flaky, with the vegetables soft and easy to digest.

Stuffed Zucchini With Brown Rice

Soft zucchini filled with mild whole grains.

Ingredients

2 medium zucchini

1 ½ cups cooked brown rice (cooked until soft)

1 teaspoon olive oil

½ small onion, finely chopped (steamed or sautéed until soft)

½ small bell pepper, chopped (steamed or sautéed)

1 small garlic clove, minced

1 medium tomato, peeled, seeded, and chopped

¼ cup cooked and mashed carrots or mild squash (to replace pecans for a softer texture)

½ teaspoon dried thyme (or mild herb like basil)

Salt and freshly ground black pepper, to taste (use sparingly)

½ cup mozzarella cheese, shredded (lightly used)

2 tablespoons Parmesan cheese, shredded (lightly used)

Instructions

Preheat the oven to 350°F (175°C). Trim the zucchinis, cut them in half lengthwise, and scoop out the pulp, leaving about ¼ inch of the zucchini shell. In a skillet, sauté the onion, bell pepper, and garlic with a small amount of olive oil until softened, then add the chopped tomato and cook for another 2 minutes. Stir in the cooked rice, mashed carrots or squash, thyme, and a pinch of salt and pepper. Mix gently until everything is combined.

Stuff the zucchini halves with the rice and vegetable mixture, pressing it gently to ensure it's evenly packed. Top with a small amount of mozzarella and Parmesan cheese. Place the stuffed zucchinis in a shallow casserole dish, cover with foil, and bake for 30 minutes. Remove the foil and bake for another 10 minutes or until the cheese is melted and slightly golden.

Black Bean and Avocado Bowl

Creamy and fiber rich.

Ingredients

¼ cup cooked black beans (drained and rinsed if canned)

¼ avocado, mashed

Optional spices: pinch of cumin, mild chili powder, or a dash of salt (to taste)

Instructions

In a small bowl, combine the mashed avocado and the cooked black beans. Stir gently to mix the two ingredients until well combined, creating a smooth, creamy texture with the beans maintaining a bit of bite. If desired, add a small pinch of cumin or mild chili powder to enhance the flavor without overwhelming the dish. A touch of salt can be added to taste, but keep it minimal to avoid overpowering the mild nature of the meal.

For a warmer dish, you can lightly heat the mixture in the microwave or on the stove until it reaches a comfortable temperature. Serve immediately for a soft, nourishing meal that's rich in fiber and healthy fats, perfect for Phase 3 recovery.

Barley and Vegetable Casserole

Hearty but gentle on digestion.

Ingredients

½ cup cooked barley

½ cup cooked vegetables (such as carrots, zucchini, or spinach)

Optional spices: pinch of dried thyme, a dash of salt, a pinch of black pepper (to taste)

Optional light dressing: 1 teaspoon olive oil or a light drizzle of vegetable broth

Instructions

Preheat the oven to 350°F (175°C). In a medium bowl, combine the cooked barley and vegetables. For seasoning, add a small pinch of dried thyme and a dash of salt and black pepper to taste. These herbs and spices are mild yet add a subtle depth of flavor without overwhelming the dish. For added moisture and gentleness, you can also drizzle 1 teaspoon of olive oil or a small amount of vegetable broth into the mixture. Stir everything together until evenly combined.

Transfer the mixture into a lightly greased casserole dish, ensuring it's spread evenly. Cover the casserole with aluminum foil and bake for 20-25 minutes, or until everything is heated through and the flavors have melded together. If you'd like a slightly crispy top, remove the foil for the last 5 minutes of baking. Serve immediately for a gentle yet hearty dish that's perfect for Phase 3 recovery.

Grilled Chicken With Barley

Lean protein paired with whole grains.

Ingredients

Sliced grilled chicken (about 4 oz, skinless and boneless)

½ cup cooked barley

½ cup cooked vegetables (such as carrots, zucchini, or spinach)

Optional spices: pinch of salt, pepper, and dried thyme (use sparingly)

1 teaspoon olive oil (optional, for extra flavor)

Instructions

Grill the chicken until tender and fully cooked, seasoning lightly with salt, pepper, and dried thyme. You can also use olive oil for a bit of extra flavor and moisture. Slice the grilled chicken into thin, bite-sized pieces for easy digestion.

While the chicken is grilling, cook the barley according to the package instructions, ensuring it is soft and tender. In a separate pan, lightly steam or sauté the vegetables (such as carrots, zucchini, or spinach) until they are soft but not overcooked, making them easier to digest. Once everything is cooked, serve the grilled chicken alongside the cooked barley and vegetables. Drizzle a small amount of olive oil over the barley and vegetables if desired. Serve immediately while warm for a simple, balanced, and gentle meal suitable for Phase 3 recovery.

Fava Bean and Hummus Bowl

Smooth and satisfying.

Ingredients

¼ cup cooked fava beans (drained and rinsed if using canned)

1 tablespoon hummus (store-bought or homemade)

Optional: 1 teaspoon olive oil (for smoothness)

Optional spices: pinch of salt, a dash of cumin or paprika (use sparingly)

Optional vegetables: finely chopped cucumber or soft-cooked zucchini (for added texture)

Instructions

In a small bowl, combine the cooked fava beans with the hummus and begin gently mashing the mixture with the back of a spoon. Continue stirring until the texture becomes smooth, creamy, and easy to scoop. If the mixture feels too thick, add a teaspoon of olive oil to create a softer, velvety consistency that blends well without becoming heavy. The goal is to achieve a mild, spreadable texture that remains easy on digestion.

Season the mixture with a very small pinch of salt and a light dash of cumin or paprika to give it a warm, subtle flavor without irritation. For added freshness and gentle texture, you can fold in a small amount of finely chopped cucumber or soft cooked zucchini, making sure the pieces are tender enough to blend smoothly. Mix carefully until everything is evenly combined, then serve immediately as a creamy, satisfying bowl that offers gentle fiber and plant based protein during Phase 3 recovery.

Whole Grain Chickpea Stir Fry

Soft stir fried vegetables with chickpeas.

Ingredients

¼ cup chickpeas (cooked or canned, drained and rinsed)

½ cup cooked vegetables (such as carrots, zucchini, or spinach)

1 teaspoon olive oil (for sautéing)

Optional spices: pinch of salt, ¼ teaspoon ground cumin, ¼ teaspoon mild paprika or turmeric (use sparingly)

1 teaspoon lemon juice (optional, for a mild zing)

Instructions

In a non-stick skillet, heat 1 teaspoon of olive oil over medium heat. Add the cooked vegetables to the skillet and sauté gently until they are warmed through and tender. If needed, add a splash of water to keep the vegetables soft and moist.

Once the vegetables are soft, add the cooked chickpeas to the skillet and stir to combine. For seasoning, add a pinch of salt, a small sprinkle of cumin, and a dash of mild paprika or turmeric for warmth and color. These spices should be used sparingly to avoid overwhelming the dish. If you prefer a mild acidity, drizzle a small amount of lemon juice over the stir fry just before serving. Stir the mixture until the flavors are well-combined and serve immediately for a mild, nourishing meal.

Salmon With Quinoa and Greens

Balanced and nourishing.

Ingredients

1 small salmon fillet (about 4 oz)

¼ cup quinoa (cooked until soft)

¼ cup soft greens (such as spinach, kale, or arugula)

Optional spices: pinch of salt, pepper, lemon zest, or dried dill (use sparingly)

1 teaspoon olive oil (for drizzling)

Instructions

Preheat the oven to 375°F (190°C). Place the salmon fillet on a baking sheet lined with parchment paper or a lightly greased pan. Drizzle with a small amount of olive oil, and season lightly with salt, pepper, and a touch of dried dill or lemon zest for a mild, aromatic flavor. Bake the salmon for 12-15 minutes, or until it is fully cooked and flakes easily with a fork.

While the salmon is baking, cook the quinoa according to the package instructions until it is soft and fluffy. In a separate pan, gently sauté the greens with a small splash of water or olive oil until they are wilted and soft. Once everything is cooked, serve the salmon with the quinoa and greens, ensuring the dish remains tender and easy to digest.

Chicken With Mixed Bean Salad

A protein and fiber combination.

Ingredients

1 small chicken breast (about 4 oz)

¼ cup mixed cooked beans (such as kidney beans, black beans, or chickpeas)

¼ cup soft vegetables (such as cooked zucchini, carrots, or spinach)

Optional spices: pinch of salt, pepper, dried basil, or dried oregano (use sparingly)

1 teaspoon olive oil (for drizzling)

1 teaspoon lemon juice or mild vinaigrette (optional, for added flavor)

Instructions

Season the chicken breast with a small pinch of salt and pepper, and cook it thoroughly on medium heat (grill, pan-fry, or bake at 375°F/190°C) until it is tender and fully cooked, approximately 6-8 minutes on each side, depending on the thickness. If desired, drizzle with a little olive oil to enhance flavor and moisture.

While the chicken is cooking, heat the mixed beans and the soft vegetables (such as cooked zucchini, carrots, or spinach) until they are warmed through. For a mild dressing, mix a teaspoon of olive oil with a small splash of lemon juice or a mild vinaigrette. Once everything is cooked, serve the chicken breast alongside the mixed beans and vegetables. Drizzle with the dressing and toss gently to combine. Serve immediately for a well-balanced, mild meal that's easy to digest and perfect for Phase 3 recovery.

Whole Grain Spaghetti With Marinara

Soft pasta with light tomato sauce.

Ingredients

1 cup cooked whole grain spaghetti (soft, not al dente)

¼ cup mild marinara sauce (smooth, no chunks)

1 teaspoon olive oil (optional, for moisture)

Pinch of salt (optional)

Safe spices: tiny pinch of dried basil or dried oregano

Optional mild flavor: ½ teaspoon grated Parmesan

Instructions

Cook the whole grain spaghetti until very soft, slightly past the usual texture, to ensure it is gentle on digestion. Drain the pasta and drizzle with a teaspoon of olive oil to keep the strands moist and easy to swallow. In a small saucepan, warm the marinara sauce over low heat; be sure it is a smooth sauce without large vegetable chunks, seeds, or spicy seasonings. Add a very small pinch of dried basil or dried oregano if you prefer a subtle herbal flavor, keeping the amount minimal so the dish stays mild.

Once the sauce is warm, pour it over the cooked spaghetti and toss gently until the pasta is evenly coated. If desired, sprinkle a very small amount of grated Parmesan on top to add softness and mild flavor. Serve the dish warm, ensuring the texture remains smooth and easy to digest. This makes a comforting Phase 3 recovery meal that introduces fiber gradually while staying stomach friendly.

SNACK AND DESSERT RECIPES

Almond and Date Energy Bites

Soft and naturally sweet.

Ingredients

½ cup soft pitted dates (about 75 g)

½ cup almonds, very finely ground (about 75 g)

1 tablespoon very finely shredded coconut (optional)

1-2 teaspoons water (only if needed to soften mixture)

Instructions

Begin by soaking the pitted dates in warm water for about 10–15 minutes until they become very soft, then drain and pat dry. Place the almonds in a pan over low to medium heat and warm them gently for just a minute or two until fragrant, being careful not to brown or over-toast them. Let them cool completely, then grind them into a very fine powder in a food processor, ensuring no large pieces remain. Add the softened dates to the food processor and blend until a smooth, sticky paste forms. If the mixture feels too dry or crumbly, add a teaspoon of water and blend again, repeating only if absolutely necessary.

Once the mixture is soft and well combined, divide it into small portions and roll each into a bite sized ball using your palms. The texture should be smooth, tender, and easy to chew, without any noticeable nut chunks. If you enjoy coconut, roll the balls lightly in finely shredded coconut for a gentle coating. Chill for 10-15 minutes to help them set, or enjoy immediately for a soft, naturally sweet Phase 3 friendly snack.

Fresh Fruit Salad Cup

Soft pieces of digestion friendly fruit, lightly combined for a soothing and fiber rich snack.

Ingredients

½ cup assorted Phase 3 safe soft fruits, such as:

Ripe banana slices

Soft ripe peach (peeled)

Ripe pear (peeled)

Soft berries (raspberries, blueberries, strawberries)

Ripe mango

Soft melon (cantaloupe or honeydew)

Instructions

Peel and finely chop all Phase 3 friendly fruits into small, soft pieces, removing any seeds, tough skins, or fibrous parts, and gently toss them together in a small bowl just until lightly combined so the fruit stays intact and tender. Serve immediately at room temperature or slightly chilled for a soothing, easy to digest fiber rich snack.

Soft Seasoned Chickpeas

Creamy, warm, and lightly seasoned for a soothing, protein rich snack.

Ingredients

¼ cup cooked chickpeas (very soft and tender)

1 teaspoon olive oil

Pinch of salt

Pinch of mild spice (optional): paprika or turmeric

Pinch of dried herbs (optional): oregano or basil

Instructions

Warm the cooked chickpeas in a small pan over low heat and drizzle in the olive oil, stirring until they are glossy and soft. Add a tiny pinch of salt along with a very small amount of mild spice like paprika or turmeric if desired, keeping the seasoning gentle for easier digestion. Continue heating for a few minutes until the chickpeas are warmed through and lightly coated in the oil and seasoning. Serve immediately for a soft, flavorful snack that provides protein without any harsh texture, making it ideal for Phase 3 recovery.

Whole Grain Crackers With Hummus

A simple, mild fiber snack with the option to use soft homemade crackers for easier digestion.

Ingredients

Whole grain crackers (store bought or homemade soft crackers below)

1 tablespoon hummus

Optional Homemade Soft Whole Grain Crackers

Ingredients

½ cup whole wheat flour

¼ cup oat flour

2 tablespoons olive oil

¼ teaspoon salt

3 to 4 tablespoons warm water

Instructions

In a small bowl, combine the whole wheat flour, oat flour, and salt. Add the olive oil and mix until the dough becomes crumbly. Begin adding warm water one tablespoon at a time, stirring until a soft, smooth dough forms that is easy to handle without sticking. Place the dough between two sheets of parchment paper and roll it out gently until thin. Cut into small squares with a knife or pizza cutter, keeping the pieces small so they stay soft after baking.

Transfer the parchment sheet with the cut dough onto a baking tray and bake at 325°F (165°C) for 8 to 10 minutes, removing them while still soft and flexible rather than crisp. Let the crackers cool slightly; they should remain tender for easy chewing.

How to Serve

Spread the hummus lightly over the soft crackers or place it in a small dipping dish on the side. Enjoy immediately as a gentle, easy to digest Phase 3 snack that offers mild fiber without overwhelming the stomach.

Dark Chocolate Almond Bites

A small treat with texture.

Ingredients

1 square dark chocolate

Few crushed almonds

Instructions

Begin by warming the dark chocolate gently, either by microwaving it in short 10–15 second intervals or melting it slowly over very low heat on the stove. Stir the chocolate frequently to prevent overheating and ensure it stays smooth and glossy. Once melted, remove it from the heat and allow it to cool slightly so it thickens just a bit but remains pourable.

Stir in the very finely crushed almonds, making sure there are no large or hard pieces that could be difficult to digest during Phase 3 recovery. Mix until the almonds are evenly distributed, then spoon the mixture onto a small piece of parchment paper and shape it into a soft bite. Let it chill briefly in the fridge until just firm enough to hold its shape while still tender and easy to chew. Enjoy in a very small portion as a gentle, mild treat.

Pear and Raspberry Tart Cup

A soft, gently sweet tart made with a tender nut-oat crust and a smooth fruit filling.

Ingredients

For the crust

½ cup almonds (or walnuts)

¼ cup oats

4 soft dates, pitted (soak 10 minutes in warm water if firm)

1 teaspoon olive oil or melted butter

Small pinch of cinnamon (optional)

For the filling

1 ripe pear, peeled and finely chopped

¼ cup fresh raspberries

1 teaspoon honey or maple syrup

1 teaspoon lemon juice

1–2 tablespoons water

Optional topping

1–2 teaspoons melted dark chocolate (thin drizzle only)

Instructions

Begin by preparing the crust. Place the almonds, oats, softened dates, and optional cinnamon into a food processor and pulse until the mixture forms a soft, sticky dough that holds together when pressed. Lightly grease small tart molds or mini tart pans, then press the crust mixture evenly across the base and slightly up the sides to form a soft tart shell. Chill the tart shells in the refrigerator for about 15 minutes so they firm up slightly while you prepare the filling.

For the filling, add the chopped pear, raspberries, honey, and lemon juice to a small saucepan. Cook over low heat with 1–2 tablespoons of water until the fruit becomes soft, saucy, and easy to mash, about 5–7 minutes. Mash lightly to form a smooth but slightly textured fruit filling, then let it cool briefly. Spoon the fruit mixture into the chilled tart shells and spread evenly. If using the optional melted chocolate, drizzle a very thin layer on top. Chill the tarts until set and serve gently warmed or at room temperature for a soft, easy-to-digest Phase 3 dessert.

Apple Slices With Almond Butter

A soft, naturally sweet snack with gentle healthy fats.

Ingredients

1 soft ripe apple, peeled and thinly sliced

1 teaspoon smooth almond butter

Instructions

Peel the apple fully so the tougher skin is removed, then slice it into thin, even pieces so each slice stays soft and easy to chew during digestion. If the almond butter feels firm, warm it slightly so it becomes smooth and easy to spread without adding any heaviness. Arrange the thin apple slices on a small plate, keeping them slightly overlapping or fanned out so they hold their shape and remain visually appealing.

Once the almond butter is warm and creamy, drizzle it lightly over the apples or spread a thin layer across each slice for a mild, gentle flavor pairing. Serve the snack immediately while the apple is fresh and tender. The combination offers natural sweetness, healthy fats, and a soft texture that supports Phase 3 recovery without overwhelming the stomach.

Roasted Pumpkin Seeds

A light, crisp snack best enjoyed in very small amounts during Phase 3.

Ingredients

2 tablespoons pumpkin seeds

Pinch of salt

½ teaspoon olive oil

Instructions

Coat the pumpkin seeds lightly in olive oil and a small pinch of salt, then spread them out on a parchment-lined baking tray. Bake at 300°F (150°C) for about 12 to 15 minutes until very lightly crisp but not overly hard, ensuring they stay gentle enough for Phase 3 in small portions.

Let the seeds cool until just warm, and serve in a very small handful to avoid any digestive strain. The mild flavor and gentle crunch make this a safe, fiber-adding snack when eaten slowly and in moderation.

Cucumber and Carrot Sticks With Guacamole Dip

A refreshing fiber-friendly snack with soft vegetables and creamy dip.

Ingredients

¼ cup soft cucumber sticks (peeled)

¼ cup soft carrot sticks (very lightly steamed)

2 tablespoons smooth guacamole

Instructions

Peel the cucumber and cut it into soft sticks, then lightly steam the carrot sticks for 3 to 4 minutes until tender but still holding their shape. Let them cool slightly before serving so the textures remain gentle and easy to chew.

Place the guacamole in a small bowl and arrange the vegetable sticks around it. Dip gently and enjoy as a mild, refreshing Phase 3 snack that brings fiber back safely without irritating the stomach.

Pear With Cheese Slices

A soft, sweet, and creamy combination perfect for gentle digestion.

Ingredients

½ soft ripe pear, peeled and sliced

2 thin slices mild cheese (such as mozzarella or mild cheddar)

Instructions

Begin by peeling the pear completely so the tougher outer skin is removed, ensuring each bite remains soft and easy to digest. Slice the pear into thin, even wedges, choosing only the tender flesh and avoiding any firm or gritty parts. Select a mild cheese such as mozzarella, Havarti, or mild cheddar, and cut it into thin slices that blend smoothly with the natural sweetness of the pear. Keeping both components soft helps create a snack that is gentle enough for a recovering digestive system.

Arrange the pear slices neatly on a small plate and place the cheese either layered on top or served alongside, depending on your preference for texture and presentation. Serve immediately so the pear stays fresh and tender. This simple pairing of soft fruit and mild cheese provides a soothing balance of natural sugars, gentle fats, and satisfying creaminess that works well as a calming Phase 3 recovery snack.

Berry Oat Crumble Bars

A soft, warm bar made with high-fiber oats and tender berries.

Ingredients

½ cup cooked oats

¼ cup soft mixed berries

1 teaspoon honey

Instructions

Begin by combining the cooked oats and soft mixed berries in a small bowl, gently pressing the berries so they release their juices into the oats. Stir slowly until the mixture turns thick, lightly tinted with berry color, and begins to resemble a soft, cohesive dough. Add the honey and continue mixing until the sweetness blends evenly throughout, keeping the texture soft and moist so it remains easy to digest.

Transfer the mixture to a small, shallow dish and press it down firmly so it forms an even layer about one inch thick. Warm it in the oven at low heat for five to seven minutes, just enough to help it hold its shape without drying out or becoming firm. Let it cool slightly until warm and pliable, then cut it into a soft bar that you can lift gently without crumbling. Serve warm or at room temperature.

Chia Seed and Mango Pudding

A creamy pudding with tropical sweetness and gentle fiber.

Ingredients

2 tablespoons chia seeds

½ cup milk or almond milk

2 tablespoons mashed soft mango

Instructions

Mix the chia seeds and milk together in a small bowl or jar, then stir well to prevent clumping. Add the mashed mango and mix until the fruit is evenly distributed through the chia mixture.

Refrigerate overnight or for at least 4 hours until thick and pudding-like. Serve chilled for a soft, soothing, fiber-friendly treat with a mild tropical flavor.

Apple and Walnut Stuffed Dates

A naturally sweet fiber-rich bite with soft textures.

Ingredients

2 soft dates

1 tablespoon finely grated apple

1 teaspoon finely chopped soft walnuts

Instructions

Slice each date open and remove the pit, keeping the outer flesh intact and soft. Mix the grated apple with the finely chopped walnuts until the texture becomes a tender, slightly sweet filling.

Stuff the mixture into the dates and press gently to close. Serve immediately as a soft, sweet Phase 3 snack that combines fruit, healthy fats, and fiber without overwhelming the stomach.

CHAPTER 5

INTRODUCTION TO THE 31 DAY MEAL PLAN

Transitioning from individual recipes to a structured meal plan can significantly enhance the experience of eating during recovery. Instead of focusing on individual meals every day, having a pre-arranged meal plan helps you streamline your choices, creating a sense of predictability. It removes the daily uncertainty of what to eat next, and this mental relief can reduce stress, particularly during a recovery process. Many individuals find that a clear, structured meal plan allows them to stay on track with their nutritional goals and offers the consistency needed to maintain long-term digestive comfort. The process of healing becomes less daunting, knowing that each meal is designed with care and attention to the stages of recovery.

This 31-day meal plan is specifically designed to guide you through three crucial phases of recovery: the clear liquid stage, the low-fiber recovery stage, and the gradual return to a higher-fiber routine. Each phase plays an important role in reintroducing the body to foods that are easy on the digestive system, while also ensuring it receives the nutrients it needs to heal. The clear liquid stage offers hydration and rest for the digestive system, while the low-fiber recovery stage provides mild, soft foods that allow for healing without irritating the colon. As you transition into the higher-fiber phase, the meal plan gradually introduces fiber to support regular bowel movements, decrease internal pressure, and prevent future flare-ups. Throughout the plan, the meals build on the progress you have already made, ensuring that your system remains calm, nourished, and well-supported as you work towards your recovery goals.

While following the meal plan, it's important to listen to your body and make adjustments as needed. Every individual's recovery journey is unique, and flexibility is key. For instance, if you experience any discomfort or if a particular food doesn't sit well with you, it's perfectly okay to modify the plan. Eating slowly, savoring each bite, and sticking to manageable portions can help prevent any overwhelming sensations. Mild flavors, minimal seasoning, and gentle textures can also make digestion easier. Throughout the entire recovery process, hydration plays an essential role. Drinking plenty of water and staying hydrated helps keep the digestive system functioning smoothly. Additionally, taking the time to rest and prioritize self-care is equally important, as recovery isn't just about the food you consume, but also about how you care for your body. With this balanced approach grounded in mindful eating, hydration, rest, and gentle nourishment, you can approach the coming weeks of your recovery with confidence, knowing that every meal is carefully chosen to support your long-term health and comfort.

DAYS 1-3: CLEAR LIQUID PHASE

Day 1

Breakfast: Apple Cinnamon Light Broth

Lunch: Chicken Broth With Fresh Herbs

Dinner: Beef Broth Variation

Snacks: Clear Raspberry Gelatin, Peppermint Tea

Hydration: Warm lemon water throughout the day

Day 2

Breakfast: White Grape Juice Blend

Lunch: Mild Ginger Tea Broth

Dinner: Light Vegetable Broth

Snacks: Cucumber Mint Infused Water, Rose Water Gelatin

Hydration: Plain water and herbal tea

Day 3

Breakfast: Warm Lemon Honey Water

Lunch: Lemongrass Tea Cup

Dinner: Clear Mushroom Broth

Snacks: Cranberry Water Variation, Rooibos Tea

Hydration: Warm water sips through the day

DAYS 4-17: LOW FIBER RECOVERY PHASE

Day 4

Breakfast: Soft Scrambled Eggs on White Toast

Lunch: Chicken Broth With White Bread

Dinner: Baked Fish With Mashed Potatoes

Snack: Applesauce Mash

Day 5

Breakfast: Rice Cereal With Warm Milk

Lunch: Turkey Sandwich on Soft Bread

Dinner: Penne With Light Cheese Sauce

Snack: Banana and Apple Mash

Day 6

Breakfast: Soft Pancakes With Light Syrup

Lunch: White Toast With Olive Oil

Dinner: Chicken Noodle Soup Variation

Snack: Vanilla Pudding Cup

Day 7

Breakfast: Mild Rice Porridge

Lunch: Oat Porridge Variation

Dinner: Egg White Rice Bowl

Snack: Soft Pear Purée

Day 8

Breakfast: Strawberry Milk Smoothie (Strained)

Lunch: Turkey and White Bread Sandwich

Dinner: Baked Salmon With Boiled Potatoes

Snack: Rose Water Gelatin

Day 9

Breakfast: Soft Banana and Apple Mash

Lunch: Chicken Broth With Carrot Shreds

Dinner: White Pasta Salad Variation

Snack: Cucumber Water

Day 10

Breakfast: Soft Pancakes

Lunch: Mashed Potatoes With Eggs

Dinner: Turkey Sandwich on Soft Bread

Snack: Applesauce Cup

Day 11

Breakfast: Creamy Baked Egg With Mashed Potatoes

Lunch: Egg Salad With Soft Rice

Dinner: Baked Cod With Mashed Potatoes

Snack: Clear Raspberry Gelatin

Day 12

Breakfast: Cooked Carrots With Vanilla Notes

Lunch: Chicken Broth With White Bread

Dinner: Pasta With Butter and Parmesan

Snack: Strawberry Purée

Day 13

Breakfast: Rice Cereal With Warm Milk

Lunch: Turkey Soft Bread Sandwich

Dinner: Chicken Noodle Soup Variation

Snack: Soft Applesauce

Day 14

Breakfast: Mild Rice Porridge

Lunch: Egg Salad Mash

Dinner: Grilled Chicken Sandwich on Soft Bread

Snack: Vanilla Custard

Day 15

Breakfast: Soft Scrambled Eggs

Lunch: Apple and Pear Soft Blend

Dinner: Baked Salmon With Potatoes

Snack: Berry Infused Warm Water

Day 16

Breakfast: Plain Pancake With Light Syrup

Lunch: Turkey Slice Sandwich

Dinner: Penne With Light Cheese Sauce

Snack: Banana Purée

Day 17

Breakfast: Rice Porridge

Lunch: Chicken Broth

Dinner: Egg White Rice Bowl

Snack: Cucumber Mint Water

DAYS 18-31: HIGH FIBER MAINTENANCE PHASE

Day 18

Breakfast: Whole Grain Toast With Avocado Mash

Lunch: Grilled Vegetable and Quinoa Salad

Dinner: Barley and Vegetable Casserole

Snack: Fresh Fruit Salad Cup

Day 19

Breakfast: Warm Oatmeal With Mixed Berries

Lunch: Lentil Soup With Whole Grain Roll

Dinner: Salmon With Quinoa and Greens

Snack: Almond and Date Bite

Day 20

Breakfast: Chia Seed Pudding

Lunch: Chickpea Salad Sandwich

Dinner: Black Bean and Avocado Bowl

Snack: Whole Grain Crackers With Hummus

Day 21

Breakfast: Vegetable Omelet With Whole Grain Toast

Lunch: Turkey and Avocado Wrap

Dinner: Whole Grain Spaghetti With Marinara

Snack: Soft Fruit Mix

Day 22

Breakfast: Greek Yogurt With Fruit Mix

Lunch: Chickpea and Quinoa Salad

Dinner: Baked Fish With Vegetables

Snack: Roasted Chickpeas Variation

Day 23

Breakfast: Breakfast Quinoa With Fresh Fruit

Lunch: Veggie Wrap With Hummus

Dinner: Chicken With Mixed Bean Salad

Snack: Dark Chocolate Almond Bites (small portion)

Day 24

Breakfast: Raisin Bran Muffin Variation

Lunch: Vegetable Lemon Vinaigrette Bowl

Dinner: Grilled Chicken With Barley

Snack: Banana Slices

Day 25

Breakfast: Whole Grain Pancakes With Berry Compote

Lunch: Heartwarming Tomato and Lentil Soup

Dinner: Whole Grain Chickpea Stir Fry

Snack: Pear Purée

Day 26

Breakfast: Almond Butter Overnight Oats

Lunch: Corn and Spinach Salad Cup

Dinner: Salmon With Quinoa

Snack: Soft Peaches

Day 27

Breakfast: Vegetable Omelet

Lunch: Chickpea and Quinoa Bowl

Dinner: Stuffed Zucchini With Brown Rice

Snack: Fresh Fruit Cup

Day 28

Breakfast: Banana Nut Muffin Variation

Lunch: Wholemeal Pasta Salad Bowl

Dinner: Barley and Vegetable Casserole

Snack: Soft Apples

Day 29

Breakfast: Oatmeal With Fruit

Lunch: Grilled Vegetable Salad

Dinner: Chicken With Mixed Greens and Beans

Snack: Whole Grain Crackers

Day 30

Breakfast: Chia Pudding With Fruit

Lunch: Lentil Soup

Dinner: Salmon With Vegetables

Snack: Fresh Berry Cup

Day 31

Breakfast: Quinoa Breakfast Bowl

Lunch: Chickpea Salad Sandwich

Dinner: Black Bean Bowl With Soft Greens

Snack: Pear and Raspberry Tart Cup

MOVING FORWARD AFTER THE 31 DAY PLAN

Completing a full month of structured meals brings a sense of accomplishment and clarity, offering reassurance that you're on the right path to digestive healing. This meal plan has been carefully crafted to support the healing of your colon, gradually reintroducing more texture and fiber in a way that minimizes strain and discomfort. By allowing your digestive system to rest during the early stages and then gently easing it into more varied foods, you have established a solid foundation for long-term comfort. This plan was not just about following a set schedule; it was about learning what foods work best for your body, what to avoid, and how to listen to your digestive system's needs.

As you move forward beyond the 31 days, adopting gentle habits will help maintain the progress you've made. Continue to eat slowly and mindfully, choosing foods that are kind to your digestion, while also drinking plenty of water to keep your system functioning well. This combination will keep things moving smoothly and prevent any unnecessary strain on your digestive tract. It's important to monitor your symptoms and adjust as needed, remembering that it's normal for some days to feel easier than others. If you feel unsettled, it's perfectly okay to return to earlier phases of the plan for a short time to recalibrate. Your body is always communicating, so staying attuned to those signals will guide your food choices moving forward. With the routine you've built and the knowledge gained from this plan, you're now better equipped to manage any flare-ups, prevent discomfort, and enjoy your meals with confidence and mindfulness. The next chapter will provide even more helpful resources and tools to support your ongoing digestive health journey.

CHAPTER 6

BONUS TOOLS FOR DAILY SUPPORT

Helpful tools can make day to day management feel more manageable, especially when you are learning how your body reacts to certain foods. These simple guides strengthen your ability to track symptoms, plan meals, and stay consistent with your routine. Each tool is designed to support clarity, reduce stress, and bring steady progress.

SYMPTOM AND FOOD DIARY

Keeping a daily record of symptoms and meals can help you identify patterns and understand how your digestive system responds to different foods. Writing down your observations makes it easier to recognize triggers early and adjust your routine before discomfort intensifies.

Daily Tracking Page Includes:

Foods and drinks consumed

Time of meals

Energy levels

Bloating or gas

Bowel movements and comfort level

Any flare signals

Notes on stress, sleep, and hydration

Try completing the page each evening. Over time, these notes create a clear picture of what supports your comfort and what may require adjustment.

WEEKLY SHOPPING LISTS

Organizing your shopping list around the three phases can help you stay prepared. Having the right foods available reduces last minute decisions and makes meal planning smoother.

Phase 1 Essentials

Clear broths

Herbal teas

Clear fruit juices

Gelatin mixes

Electrolyte beverages

Lemon and honey

Water and flavored waters

Phase 2 Essentials

White bread

Soft cereals

Eggs

Potatoes and mashed potato ingredients

Tender fish or chicken

Low fiber fruits

Soft noodles and pasta

Milk or milk alternatives

Phase 3 Essentials

Whole grains

Fresh fruits

Cooked vegetables

Lentils, beans, and chickpeas

Yogurt

Nuts in small amounts

Healthy oils

Lean meats and fish

Use these lists as a starting point and add items that fit your preferences.

FIBER REINTRODUCTION GUIDE

Adding fiber back into your routine requires patience. Increasing fiber too quickly can cause discomfort, but a slow and steady approach encourages healthy digestion.

How to Reintroduce Fiber Safely:

Begin with soft cooked vegetables

Add small servings of fruit without skins

Introduce whole grains in half portions

Increase portions gradually over several days

Drink plenty of water throughout the day

Your body will signal when you are ready to add more. Mild fullness or extra gas can be normal at first, but sharp discomfort may mean you should slow down.

MEAL PREP TIPS FOR COMFORT

Preparing meals ahead of time can bring ease to your routine and reduce stress on busy days. Simple steps can help you stay consistent even when your schedule changes.

Supportive Tips:

Cook large batches of broth and freeze in small containers

Prepare soft vegetables and store in single servings

Keep cooked grains in the fridge for quick meals

Assemble simple snacks like yogurt cups or fruit purées

Store safe condiments and oils in easy reach

A little preparation can help you stay comfortable and prevent reaching for foods that may irritate your system.

GENTLE LIFESTYLE HABITS

Small lifestyle habits can support digestion just as effectively as diet changes. When practiced regularly, these habits can help reduce the frequency of flare ups and maintain balance.

Helpful Daily Habits:

Take a short walk after meals

Drink water steadily throughout the day

Practice slow, relaxed breathing when stressed

Maintain a predictable eating schedule

Get enough sleep each night

Avoid skipping meals

These simple routines help your digestive system work smoothly and reduce unnecessary strain.